# THE WHEELS ON THE BUS ARE

## *Square*

---

## EDUCATION UNDER FIRE

*The Secret Life of a First Grade Teacher*

## LISA GRAHM

# Table of Contents

To the two most competent, kindest Principals with whom I ever worked and to all of my students at *Paul Robeson Elementary School.*

# Acknowledgments

To the grade school Librarian who cheered while I tried to read every book in the library.

To the 6th grade teacher who taught me to write for reader understanding.

To the Funeral Director who helped me understand the value of grief.

To every student who forced me to learn to teach to their needs.

To my 'other half' who carefully solved the computer typing problems.

To Theo Madden and his team at www.BakeMyBook.com whose editing efforts and design work brought this manuscript to life.

# About the author

Lisa Grahm is a retired First Grade Teacher with a Bachelor of Arts degree in Sociology and a Master's Degree in Urban Education. She lives in South Florida with her husband, two small rescue dogs, and a sleepy black cat. Writing about Life's Events was always a favorite past time. This is her first publication.

# Introduction

A first grade classroom in an inner-city school was always an adventure. The more years I taught, the more I realized that someone ought to record some of them. The real classroom was a far cry from the teaching examples described by Colleges of Education.

Careful planning was an invaluable aid, and then there were times when careful planning was not nearly enough. This is a memoir of those times. First grade teaching consumed most of my life. My classroom and its children took every ounce of planning, forethought, observation, insight, knowledge, physical strength, and patience I could muster – day after day after day. I worked from my heart, doing more than my job. It was fun, but also exhausting, as well as imperative for my children's success.

# Foreword

Riding this bus are the First Graders of Room 212, their teacher, and an assortment of school-affiliated adults. As teaching and learning continue throughout another school year, both academic and real-life lessons are learned. The ride is often hilarious, sometimes sad, and always truthful.

Come ride beside the teacher for insights into the real world of inner-city public school classrooms. You will see the role POVERTY plays everywhere, and by year's end, you too, will enjoy the pleasures of First Graders' enormous success.

Names and dates have been changed; all similarities are coincidental.

*Lisa Grahm*
*2022*

# 1. COMBAT PAY

'Combat Pay', she called it: the salary earned by inner-city teachers. No one could pay her enough to do what she did every day. She considered it the most difficult and the most important job of her life. Driving to work that morning, she noticed the blowing paper and empty plastic bottles crackling in the gutter; the abandoned buildings looked emptier and more ominous than ever. Headlights reflected off the shiny wet street into her eyes. She shivered. There were fifty-four more blocks of decay and discouragement to go.

Stopped at a red light, she had just settled comfortably to wait when she saw a small cinnamon tabby sitting under the portico of an ornate brown brick building. Once a private gourmet club, its large, leaded-glass oak doors and intricate gray trim now decorated a dormitory for the State's delinquent teenage learners. Eight stories above, protected by overhanging eaves, molded concrete Muses watched over the entrance benignly. The kitten sat calmly in the rain, observing students walk to class.

Directly across the street was a large city high school. From her car, she watched the students: book bags on heads, a few umbrellas, colorful headscarves,

1

eyes scanning the uneven sidewalk. No one stopped to pick up the little kitten. The traffic light changed to green; she had to go – hers was the first car in line at the traffic light.

"Damn! YOU should have picked up that kitten. You had time to jump out and grab it. What were you thinking?" Traffic was so congested, she dared not try to look back.

"You just *watched* it happen: passively, you idiot! It's like every other failure in this city; you didn't ACT! You allowed it to happen."

Her mother always chastised her own self: called herself derogatory names and scolded herself when she failed to do something she thought she ought to have done. She had watched her mother do the same for so many years that unconsciously, Grahm did it too, to herself. She steered her silver Hyundai onto Fifth Avenue and settled back into the driver's seat again. Some classical music might make her feel better. It would take another fifteen minutes to return to the corner where the kitten had been. She needed that fifteen minutes to get to school on time. She reached around the headlight knob to push the radio's ON button. Out of the surround-sound speakers, Saint-

Saëns' *G Minor Sherzando* played out happily to her sinking spirits. Her heart beat a little faster. If she knew how to write music, she would have written this one. It was HER song. When she needed a lift, she loved to hear this piece of music. She was surprised it was playing this morning. She adjusted the volume to hum along. That's what she loved about Saint-Saëns; Mendelssohn too; their melodies were SO 'singable'.

The pain she felt for the kitten was waning. She hoped the little tabby would survive. There was nothing more she could do. She had missed her chance to save it. Somehow it seemed a contradiction to drive through the most neglected, poorest neighborhoods. At the same time, she, well-fed and well-clothed, warm and comfortable, could enjoy European Classical music while driving the 18 miles to work. It was a sort of oxymoron: like a neighborhood on Poverty Street where large elegant mansions stood in every lot.

This music seemed to reflect to her her own life; happy, followed by lightly changed seconds, then minors, and back to happy again. She enjoyed it. How falsely safe she knew she was: riding in a small car outfitted with seat belts and airbags. A rock through the windshield could ruin her life forever. Like the distant chance of nuclear accidents, or bombs, which she chose to ignore, the violent possibilities in the streets she drove, she also ignored. Her music softened that threat. Caution made her drive in the center lane: slowing for red lights until they turned green, watching behind and beside her car, observing every activity in front. She hoped she could avoid running over someone who tried to halt her car or get into it. Nothing good could ever come from a forced stop on these streets.

Inevitably, real-time returned. In another few blocks, she would start her school day. As she pulled onto the school's asphalt driveway, her headlights picked up a picture of the cook, Lorene, staring out the small window in the Boiler Room entrance door.

"I've taught here for four years, and I've never seen her there before," she exclaimed, puzzled.

Lorene's face disappeared from the window. She pulled her car into its usual parking space, turned off the engine, and stretched behind her seat to gather her books and lesson plans. With her empty hand, she reached to open the driver's door.

"Miss?"

A wrinkled, bearded, too thin, very dirty face was two inches from her window. She panicked; visions of crack cocaine, heroin addiction, alcoholism, desperation, insanity, sociopathic murder and starvation flashed before her. She was totally unprepared for this moment... and scared.

"Do you have a few dollars you could spare?"

He seemed so needy, so quietly appealing. She was trembling. Safety warnings marched through her mind:

NEVER let anyone see your money.

NEVER look street people in the eye.

IGNORE beggars.

GET AWAY as fast as you can.

She did not know what to do. A piece of her wanted to help, yet another piece warned her NOT to. Did he have a gun? She paused to think, only to find she couldn't. She rolled down the car window a scant half-inch.

"I'm afraid of you," she confided.

His face fell.

"I'd like to help you though."

"Oh, yes Ma'am." A smile spread across his emaciated face. "I wouldn't hurt you. Don't be afraid."

He put out his hand while she reached into her pocket. At that moment, Lorene came bursting through the Custodian's door: feet planted wide, short and stocky built, she shook a fist at the beggar. In her most forceful Lunch Room voice, she yelled, "You get the fuck outta here and don't you NEVER bother our teachers no more! Get outta here! GO!"

He went! Just like that, he left. He couldn't get to the sidewalk fast enough. He raced down Fifth Avenue, never looking back.

At that time, Grahm didn't know what the neighborhood knew; Lorene always packed a pistol.

She DID know that she needed a plan. Something similar could easily happen again. She, with a Bachelor's degree and a Master's degree couldn't think clearly enough to restart her car's engine, put the gear shift into **DRIVE**, and simply leave the scene.

*"DUMB!... and you've got all that education?"*

# 2. KIERRA

This neighborhood was the city's poorest, most crime-ridden area: grimy, dilapidated dwellings, littered streets, graffiti-covered buildings, a bar on every block, SUVs blaring rap music, nightly gunshots and obvious illegal drug deals openly going down on side streets everywhere.

To Kierra, this was home; she loved it; this neighborhood was all she knew. Kierra walked it and played in it every day. But its main street could be deadly. In this neighborhood, traffic laws were irrelevant to drivers who had nothing to lose. People and animals who stepped off the sidewalk were injured daily. Everyone who managed to survive, learned to check traffic in both directions *before* they crossed.

Kierra lived a few blocks from the school. Her grandmother had legal custody of Kierra and was raising her. Because of economic difficulties, she was forced to live in Government Subsidized Housing (aka 'The Projects'). Her grandmother was an old-school Southern Lady. Like all well-bred southern ladies, Grandmother fixed her hair, put on clean clothes, and donned a dressy hat and gloves when she went out. Unbeknownst to Kierra, she frequently walked to school to check on her grandchild. She had already lost Kierra's mother to street drugs; she was not about to lose her daughter's daughter too. Kierra would behave properly at church and school. Like her guardian, she would be neatly dressed in clean, well-fitting clothes. She would not embarrass Grandmother. Kierra understood that her grandmother had eyes in the back of her head and ears tuned directly into the school. So she behaved accordingly.

Unlike the other first-grade girls, Kierra was taller, her new front teeth straight and in place; her long arms and legs far less 'ashy' than the other children's dry, flaking skin. Kierra's hair was cut short and straightened; it framed her face in soft dark ringlets. The other girls wore carefully crafted squares of hair from which skinny little braids erupted. These wisps of braids were secured with rubber bands and decorated with colorful beads. A tight braid job could be made to last at least a week. Kierra's hair was straightened and styled every morning.

Kierra carefully stayed on Grandmother's good side. Grandmother's word was law, and she *always* kept her word.

This is the story of one of many encounters with

Kierra.

...........

## COACHING KIERRA

Every Thursday morning, a special reading teacher spent the allotted ninety-minute Language Literacy period in Ms. Grahm's classroom. A Primary Reading Program sponsored by the AFL/CIO Teachers' Union was being tested at several elementary schools nationwide; Robeson was one of them. This special reading teacher was a fellow teacher from another school who had applied for and won a 'coaching' position for the duration of the program's testing period. Her job was to ensure that classroom teachers were correctly and consistently *using* this reading program. Ms. Grahm figured the teacher was part 'coach' and part snitch, although Coach adamantly protested she was 'only there to help'.

Coach *modeled* what she considered appropriate management techniques and answered teacher questions. She reported to her supervisors: locally and nationally. She and the classroom teacher 'Team Taught'. Grahm's students never knew Coach's main purpose was to supervise their teacher. The greatest thing about this reading program was that it actually

*WORKED*. Parts of it directly addressed early illiteracy and contained the missing pieces of the District's previous early reading instruction. Teachers are obliged to teach a detailed, assigned curriculum for every subject. Coach taught this new curriculum exactly within the time frame allocated and exactly as it was scripted in its Teacher Guide. Exceptions of any kind were not tolerated.

That October morning, the coach wanted to finish her ninety-minute lesson with a story. One child at a time, sometimes two: she called them to come sit in front of her on the floor.

Ronell was less than happy to sit on the floor.

"My daddy tole me I can't get dirty," he grumped when she called him to sit beside her.

Coach put her finger to her lips. "I only speak to children who remember to raise their hands to speak."

Ronell raised his hand and repeated, "My daddy tole me…"

She put her finger to her lips again, "Wait for me to call on you."

Ronell put his hand down.

"You may come up now, Ronell."

He sat stoically.

"Oh! I guess Ronell cannot hear me," she feigned. "We'll try again later." She turned her attention to another child.

Ronell lifted his desk lid. He peered inside. This situation called for some paste!

When Coach had the children gathered around her, she wiggled herself taller, folded her fingers together, and placed her hands on her lap.

"When I read you a story, I expect you to sit up straight, with your hands in your lap, like this." She looked around at the group, an encouraging smile pasted on her lips. "Look at Kierra; that is exactly the way I want you to sit."

Kierra sat tall and straight: a mirror image of Coach's posture and facial expression.

"Ronell, would you care to join us now? Quietly." Coach admonished.

Ronell didn't answer.

She waited a few seconds.

"Well, maybe next time," she acquiesced. "You may sit at your desk for now."

She turned her attention to read to the children in front of her. When the story was finished, she asked reading comprehension questions about this story of a dog whose next-door neighbor lady sang loud and long and poorly. Worst of all, the neighbor lady opened the window when she sang.

The students were getting restless. It was nearly lunchtime, and they were tired of being coached. The concrete floor was cold and dirty.

"Wasn't that a good story?"

"Ye-e-s," they chorused.

"Now we get to draw a picture of the dog and write a sentence about him. I will give you ONE piece of paper to do this, so work carefully. If you make a mistake, use the other side. Remember, you get ONE piece of paper. Please return quietly to your seats."

She reached under her chair for the stack of drawing paper she had placed there earlier. As each child walked past her, she handed out a piece of paper.

"I like the way Allan remembered to say, 'Thank you,' when he took his paper. Good job, Allan."

"David, you raised your hand? Yes, you may sharpen your pencil. Thank you for remembering how to ask." The room was quiet except for the shuffling of feet and papers.

Kierra got out of her seat, paper in hand, to tell the coach she needed another piece of paper; she had 'messed up'.

"Use the other side," Coach advised.

"I already did," whined Kierra.

"Well, then you will have to fix one of the sides. We get ONE piece of paper, remember?"

Kierra stomped back to her desk. She sat down and threw her paper on the floor. "I ain't doin' it," she said. "What kinda school is this, anyway? You can't even get one piece of paper around here." She put her head down on her desk.

Coach and Ms. Grahm were each supervising half the room to praise children's artwork and to encourage sentence writing.

"Pierre, this is wonderful. Look, boys and girls." Coach held up his drawing for all to see. Turning to Pierre, she said, "You need to write your sentence, and then you will be finished." She paused for a moment, feigning deep thought. "Boys and girls, you know, if you don't finish this activity, I'll have to give you a zero. I KNOW no one wants a ZERO."

Kierra kept her head down for a few more minutes. She gave a loud, theatrical sigh, then got out of her chair and bent down to pick up her paper from the floor. Bright-eyed, the glimmer of a brilliant idea lit up her face. She sat down to work on her paper. With one arm wrapped around it, her head bent close to it; she covered her drawing. When she was finished, she sat up very straight to wave her paper at the teacher.

"Yes, Kierra," said Coach.

"I'm done."

"I'm finished," Coach corrected. "That's very good, Kierra. I'm glad you decided you didn't want a zero. You may show me your work. Please bring it here."

Kierra walked to the back of the room where Coach and Ms. Grahm were standing. She handed her paper to Coach. On the paper, Kierra had carefully drawn trees and flowers and grass. A round, orange sun shone from a top corner. She had drawn the sky in a blue band across the top of the paper. Front and center, she had drawn a brown spotted dog, which was unmistakably urinating; one leg raised, with a single bright yellow line angled forward from his raised back leg down to the grass.

"What's this?" Coach pointed.

"Oh, that? That's sunshine," Kierra answered innocently.

"Well, then, you need to color all of this background yellow," instructed Coach. She handed the paper back to Kierra.

Kierra skipped joyfully back to her seat. She had illustrated her point.

Ms. Grahm always wondered whether Coach understood that she and her reading lesson had just been HAD by a six-year-old.

# 3. GIVING THANKS

It was Ms. Grahm's first year of teaching. She cried the forty-five minutes' drive to work and the forty-five minutes home every day. *TO work,* for not knowing how to manage her classroom and *FROM work,* for doing it wrong. At night, she had a recurring nightmare in which her 32 third grade students relentlessly climbed over rows and rows of classroom desks to **GET** her while she stood alone at the front of the classroom, powerless. Her greatest fear was that someone would find out that she wasn't really a teacher; she didn't know how to manage a classroom. $10,000, 86 semester hours in the College of Education, and a State Teaching Certificate were for naught.

In teacher's jargon, all those early, painful classroom experiences are known as 'paying your dues'. By the end of November, she had paid the learn-to-be-a-successful-teacher club three months of 'dues'.

She used every creative theory known to the University's College of Education (and then some) to plan her lessons for her students. Nothing was very effective. Her every effort was sabotaged by these same children who most needed the knowledge she tried so hard to impart. Discouraged but undaunted, she persisted. Surely there was SOME way to reach the students who didn't *want* to be at school.

Annie Goodgame taught her the first, *most* important lesson.

Annie was a barely literate third grader. She was small for her age, dainty and pretty in dirty, hand-me-down dresses. She could draw painstakingly detailed pictures sophisticated for an eight-year-old; of people, of still life, of anything she chose, but she could not read.

She could not remember the names or sounds of letters or even written words; any words, no matter how short. She could repeat information immediately after receiving it. Yet thirty seconds later, it was forgotten.

Ms. Grahm had been working hard and consistently with Annie for three months. Nothing worked with her; flashcards, writing practice, finger play, and three-page simple books. NOTHING!

Grahm was heartbroken but kept trying to help Annie anyway, often hiding her tears while working relentlessly. Annie never did learn to read that year. Only later did Ms. Grahm learn about the effects of Fetal Alcohol Syndrome on the developing brains of children. In June, she would refer Annie for psychological evaluation.

On the Tuesday night before Thanksgiving, novice teacher Grahm had stayed up late to design paper Pilgrim hats and Indian feathers for her students to wear on Wednesday in honor of the holiday. For reasons she didn't understand, this  school population seemed to care little about Thanksgiving. She had planned to incorporate a corn chips and grape juice 'feast' as part of a history lesson. Thanksgiving could be fun and certainly an important Thank You. But *NO ONE* wanted to be a Pilgrim, except a few little girls who were fond of their teacher. Annie was one of them. All of the boys and the remainder of the girls wanted to be Indians.

Years later, when assigned to an Afrocentric Magnet School, exposed to American history from an African perspective, it became evident why neither Native Americans nor African slaves trusted English colonists, particularly Pilgrims. Annie summed it up succinctly.

"Ms. Grahm, you is a nice lady, but you is TOO white!"

...........

As her experience and teaching improved, especially her knowledge of Black History, Grahm began to

18

understand the enormous ramifications of Annie's statement. Annie was absolutely correct. Blatant racism was obvious, but Grahm hadn't recognized the subtlety at other levels in which racism influenced U.S. culture.

But Annie did.

Twenty years later, retired from teaching, the memory of Annie's words continued to influence Grahm's every interaction. She would make it her goal to never again be TOO WHITE.

...........

*You changed my life. I remember you with affection and respect.*

*Thank you, Annie.*

# 4. RAGS to RICHES

That day, the music teacher was absent, which meant Ms. Grahm would have to teach her children forty minutes of music during the assigned music period. Normally, students and teacher trouped through the hallway (ALWAYS orderly and silent; otherwise, the teacher was a BAD teacher!) to the other end of the building, where the Music Room was situated.

Did you ever try to get a roomful of six-year-olds to walk *anywhere* 'silently', let alone 'walk'? Six-year-olds are busy, distractable little beings; life is their playground.

She got her students to *walk* from one end of the building to the other by being African Kings and Queens; heads held high. The girls with their hands clasped behind their backs and the boys with arms folded across their chests. There was a method to her madness; clasped hands kept them close to their owner's body; royal, respectable *AND* inoperable(!) Nobody touched anybody else.

Grahm had Kufis, and colorful head wraps for each child, which she had sewn for them on her old treadle machine. A Nigerian friend had taught her how to do a dressy 'butterfly', which she made to wrap around her little girls' heads; the boys got to choose assorted African hats called *Kufis*. Though, African garb was saved for *Harambee* assemblies to keep the headgear relatively clean and almost wrinkle-free. Thus, everyday trips through the halls required a regal attitude without headgear. When they walked to Specials, she had them pretend to be Kings and Queens because, for those few minutes, they *were!*

Grahm's room was not equipped with a piano, drums, or other handheld instruments. She was a musician by hobby, not by training. She was definitely NOT a Music Teacher. A tape deck, a variety of musical tapes, and enthusiastic children who anticipated a fun time with their teacher would work well for today. She didn't even mind missing her planning period. She already knew what she would do with them for forty minutes (it would go quickly), AND she didn't have to worry about their behavior through the long hallways.

King or not, Jared was notorious for skipping out of line to walk next to a friend or running to the front of the line so he could be 'first'. Whoever was at the front of the line would shove him or complain loudly, and the hallway misbehavior would begin.

Today, she had Jared and all her students right where she wanted them; in their seats, in their room.

*"Piece of cake!"* she thought happily.

For the past few days, a litter of four blond puppies had been following some of the children to school and stayed there all day until they were dismissed. At 3:00, the puppies tagged along as the children walked home for the night, only to return for another day at school the next morning.

Outside, after breakfast, puppies lapped the morning's milk and cereal, which leaked from under the cafeteria dumpster and played in and out of plastic playground equipment until the first group of children came outside for lunch recess.

But, back to the classroom. A tape player and stack of tapes always sat on a small, low wood table at the front of Grahm's room. She used music often, daily in fact, to signal her children instead of ringing a bell or flashing the light switch. That day, Grahm was ready with a tape to teach her students a new song.

"Ok, boys and girls. Feet on the floor, hands on desks, eyes up here. Listen to this."

She pushed the 'PLAY' button. Grandmotherly, curly, gray-haired Ms. Grahm, dressed in a skirt and

22

jacket, stood smiling in front of them. She was READY to sing with them; her enthusiasm was contagious.

From the tape player at the front of the room, a lighthearted singer sang.

Ms. Grahm pushed the OFF button.

"Ok, boys and girls, let's try the first line. Sing with me."

"I've got a dog; he's very small."

"Whoa, you're GOOD! Sing it again."

A little more sure of themselves, they sang again, louder this time.

The song continued about the little dog's fat tummy and how it almost touched the ground when he walked.

Her students smiled and sang with enthusiasm. She knew they could picture this little dog. Not only did he have a fat tummy, but he also wobbled when he walked.

"Listen again." She sang them the first two lines together."Ok, you try."

While they sang, she quickly scribbled the first four lines of the song on the chalkboard behind her. By the end of the forty minutes, she had them singing the entire song, complete with body motions. They tossed their heads and wagged a hand behind their behinds. They shook their hips when the song described the dog's walk. They put a hand over their heart to sing, "I love my dog, and he loves me." The melody was simple and repetitive; her children memorized it quickly.

"Ok, children, now stand up to sing it." With great gusto, they sang, accompanied by wig-wags and swinging hips. Grahm was pleased; music class was a happy success. "We'll sing our song for Mrs. Harris one of these days; she'll be proud of you too. In fact, maybe we can stop at her office on the way to lunch today."

*She knew better than to add, "Wouldn't that be fun?" Their response would be over the top: standing up, visiting others, talking, smiling, touching, laughing. It was easier for classroom management to keep them seated and quiet. She always offered them a treat, which they KNEW was coming any minute, when she kept them quiet longer than usual.*

*Today it would be a piece of Double Bubble gum. Chewing burned nervous energy AND delayed conversations.*

"Now remember, boys and girls, we HAVE to throw out the gum before we leave for lunch. Deonte, remind me."

"You already know this, but anyone who touches their gum with fingers LOSES it. So I wouldn't blow bubbles if I were you. VERY *small ones,* **maybe**," she reconsidered aloud.

*What good is bubble gum if you can't blow bubbles?*

"We've already had the discussion about pinworms and dirty hands…"

"We KNOW, Ms. Grahm," spoke up Kierra.

"Nasty." "Yuck." They all chorused.

Grahm walked down each row, passing out wrapped pieces of Grape Double Bubble.

"Keep the paper wrapper so you can wrap your chewed gum before you throw it in the wastebasket," she reminded them.

Every child said, "Thank you."

*Of course, it only took the first child to remember to say the thank you, and the rest copied. They loved Ms. Grahm's praise and knowing they were 'polite'. And it always pleased her to see that they remembered this very important piece of good manners. She was proud of them and proud of herself.*

"We'll read while you chew," she told them. "Today's story is another about Karlie and Kara."

She pulled up a blond, wooden teacher chair to sit in while the children settled into their desks to listen. A few minutes into the story, she knew they would trickle up front to sit closer to her and the pictures.

At the end of the story, Deonte reminded her about the gum disposal. With their gum thrown out, she got them to the bathroom before lunch, and while the children were still seated in the gym, she walked outside for a breath of sunshine and fresh air.

Something caught the corner of her eye over by the dumpster.

THERE HE WAS!

Alone, gobbling down toast and donuts, lapping up milk, and wagging his tail. She walked over to inspect that small, hungry, honey-colored piece of dogdom. Squatting down to his level, she clicked her tongue and called,

"Here, Puppy, Puppy, Puppy."

His long, skinny, hairless tail wagged faster.

"C'mon Little Guy, let me see you. Come here," she coaxed.

The puppy trotted toward her. She was thrilled, and he didn't shy when she reached to touch him. She picked him up and held him close. He wiggled and licked happily while she walked toward her car.

"Thanks, Little Guy; I need some puppy love. I'm stealing you," she told him. "You'll die in this neighborhood, and so will your brothers and sisters. You can't survive on scraps, and dirty water and the cars on Fifth Avenue. You are my prize: a gift from Paul Robeson. I need a good dog, and you need a home.

She unlocked her car and placed him on the back-seat floor. "I'll be back in two hours," she promised, "DON'T tear up my car!"

She left school earlier than usual that day to take the puppy to the vet before his office closed. She walked directly to the parking lot after she got her 'bus students' on their buses. She went to her car and prepared to hold her nose to clean up feces. Half expecting to find a gnawed-on steering wheel, she found a dirty, patchy-haired puppy contentedly snoozing on the driver's seat. He crawled eagerly into her lap during the forty-minute drive home, and he never got car sick.

Home now, she scooped up the puppy, careful to support his rear end with her forearm, and carried him into the kitchen. Her youngest daughter came running downstairs.

"Hi, Mom! You're home early… Oh my god! What is *that*?" She came close to examine the creature in her mother's arms. "Look, it's a rat dog! There's no hair on its tail. Mo-om, it's missing hair all over."

The puppy put out his tongue to lick her.

"Yew!" she pulled her hand away.

"Rose," her mom reminded her. "It's not his fault he's neglected and starving." She added, "Want to come with me to Dr. Bronson's tonight?"

"Yeah, sure. Where did you find the dog?"

Grahm told her about the Wags song and the puppy at the dumpster.

"Aww." "Put him down, Mom; I'll watch him."

At the vet's, the techs oohed and aahed over Grahm's new 'rescue'. He was remarkably filthy and balding.

Toward the end of Dr. Bronson's exam, he told them the puppy had Demodectic Mange, every worm known to dogs, ear mites, and fleas. The mange would be difficult to get rid of, but not impossible. Wags received his first puppy shots, worm capsules, mange cream, and a topical flea killer. Dr. Bronson scrubbed out the ear mites with a Q tip dipped in Ivermectin.

"What do I owe you for all this?" asked Ms. Grahm. She and Dr. Bronson had been friends for thirty years. He was fresh out of Vet School when she brought him her first dog, and Dr. Bronson had treated all of her many animals for many years.

"The puppy is a rescue, right?"

"Right."

"He needs a bath and good food, and he'll be fine. Keep after that mange, though. There is no charge."

"I'll see you in a month; he'll need his second shots. We don't charge for rescues."

Sometime during the first night in his new home, Wags needed to go outside to be excused. He had never lived inside a house, so he wasn't 'trained' yet, but he did something pretty unique for a puppy. He found the cats' litter box, jumped into it, and did his business in the cat box.

"Mom, he's a keeper."

'For sure!" Ms. Grahm said.

No one in the family quite understood why, but over time, "Wags'" name became "Waggedy". The mange disappeared. His hair returned and instead of looking muttly, he began to resemble a purebred Belgian Tervuren: medium-sized height, black mask, standing ears, with a thick, honey-colored coat. The "rat" dog now looked like a model for the American Kennel Club, handsome and proud.

Wags was probably the smartest, most loyal dog Ms. Grahm had ever owned. She was convinced the dog knew he had been rescued. A day or two after she took him home with her, his litter mates disappeared. No one at school ever saw any of them again. She was glad she had taken the puppy when she did.

Ms. Grahm had an old van she drove to run errands and go shopping. Country living on country roads was hard on cars. She also kept the Hyundai, which she drove to work or somewhere special. Her favorite memory of Wags was a picture of him, sitting at attention on the hood of the 'good' car, facing the highway, eagerly watching for her to come home.

She knew, without a doubt, that there was nothing like a good dog in the world! He was always a happy memory of her Paul Robeson years.

"I love Wags, and he loves me!"

# 5. WHEATIES, BREAKFAST of CHAMPIONS

One cold, rainy February morning, Ms. Grahm walked her students down the front stairs by the main entrance to their Gym Class around the corner. They passed a dad who had brought his son late to school and loudly insisted that his son be given breakfast immediately. Hungry children were always fed, but breakfast supplies were transferred from the gym, where all meals were served every morning when classes began.

The son was directed to the kitchen to be served. When the son returned with a Styrofoam tray of breakfast food, his dad affectionately rubbed the boy's head and told him he better get to class.

Dad hung around the hallway when his son left, like he was reluctant to leave. He seemed to be complaining to himself, but not loud enough for anyone to get the gist of his complaints. He wandered, circling the foyer, and talking to himself.

Ms. Grahm dropped her students off for gym and proceeded next door to the Parent Room. Lorene's (remember the cook peering out the Custodian Door?

The one who packed a gun to school every day?) daughter was Mrs. Carter, the Parent Liaison, who wore many hats on any given day. That day, the Attendance Officer was absent; Mrs. Carter was collecting Attendance Reports in addition to doing her Liaison job. Ms. Grahm needed to give her Room 212's Attendance Sheet. Dad entered the Parent Room immediately behind Ms. Grahm, who was waiting for Mrs. Carter to finish a telephone conversation. While waiting, she watched Dad bop and weave, muttering his way around the room's perimeter.

Whenever the kitchen had too many delivery boxes to fit in the storeroom, the excess was kept in the Parent Room across the hall from the kitchen. A one-week supply of breakfast cereal for 400 children was stacked eye-high along one wall.

"I see you got Cheerios," Dad said, "an Shredded Wheat." "An you got Frosted Flakes!" He pointed to the boxes of Sugar Corn Pops, "Yeah man, that's my kinda cereal!"

Mrs. Carter nodded in agreement, "They ARE good," she agreed. She put down the phone.

Dad was still commenting on the cereal when Ms. Grahm left the room. She handed Lorene her room's

Lunch Count on her way past the kitchen. She was relieved to go. The short, skinny young dad was acting very strange, making her uncomfortable. She walked quickly down the hall toward the classroom stairs.

The son was the spitting image of his father. He walked like him, and he looked like him. She also wondered if maybe the kid's 'old man' was a druggie. She kept walking and thinking until it suddenly dawned on her what was happening and why. The insight made her sad for her insensitivity and sadder for the dad's predicament. She suddenly realized that this young dad was hungry. He had probably brought his son in late on purpose. He walked inside with him, hoping to share his son's breakfast, but they were not serving in the gym by the time he and his son arrived. When his son was sent to the kitchen to get his breakfast, Dad didn't follow. He couldn't eat in the kitchen; the kitchen was too small. Someone would see him, and he would be embarrassed. Plus, he didn't want his son to know how hungry he was. That was what he was complaining about in the foyer. He went to the Parent Room because that was where parents were supposed to go. He saw all the food boxes along the wall when he got there. If he said how much he liked to eat a particular cereal, perhaps someone would offer him some. He was too hungry to ask directly. He couldn't risk a flat-out NO. He was hanging around, hoping someone would notice, but no one did. Instead, they agreed that it tasted good, completely missing his veiled hints.

But maybe they weren't missed. Lorene was about to enter the Parent Room when Grahm handed her the Lunch count. Did she know? Did the daughter, Mrs. Carter, know? Were they waiting for Ms. Grahm to leave?

Grahm kept graham crackers, yogurt, and juice in her room for emergencies. He was welcome to anything she had.

She turned around and practically RAN back to the kitchen. When she got to the main hall: to the foyer, Lorene was walking away from the front door, which she had just shut tightly to be sure it locked.

"Lorene, WAIT!"

Huffing and puffing, Ms. Grahm caught up with her. "That dad. You know, the one who brought his son in late?" Lorene watched her, amused. Grahm wasn't sure Lorene knew *who* she meant.

"You know, the one who was in the Parent Room, reading all the cereal boxes?" Lorene still didn't say anything.

"I think he was hungry, and he was afraid to ask." Grahm adds, "I've got food in my room he can have."

Lorene smiled. She leaned her head close to Grahm's and quietly said, "I already took care of him. That's who just went out the door."

"You fed him?"

"I fed him."

"How did you know, Lorene? The way he kept moving around, I thought he was high. And it scared me."

"After a while, you just know," she said gently.

Grahm felt like hugging her. Instead, she said simply, "I'm SO glad!"

"I do what I gotta do, Grahm." Grahm *did* hug her. "You GO, Girl!"

Lorene walked back to the kitchen while Grahm walked toward her classroom.

If Lorene were caught giving food away, she would instantly lose her job. FDA rules about subsidized school food items were rigid. No one could have government-subsidized school lunch foods but eligible children. The rules were designed to prevent abuses and ensure that the children for whom the food was intended actually got it. All of it. The food may not leave the lunchroom in pockets or purses and cannot be taken home to eat later. If a child does not eat or want his portion, it must be thrown out.

The amount of waste was horrendous. Giving leftovers away was risky business; it was a violation of Federal Law. Considering the hunger in the neighborhood, the letter of the law was counterproductive. Throwing out untouched, good and clean food was an incomprehensible waste. Each building solved that problem in its own way. One day per month, when Dietary Supervisors from 'Downtown' were present in the building, the rules were strictly followed. But on all the other days, clean, cooked, individually wrapped and untouched fresh food items were the 'perk' which attracted women from the neighborhood to seek the underpaid Lunch Aid job. Most Principals gave them tacit permission to take untouched food home, which the kids refused to eat. Children were instructed to place their unwanted food items in the center of their table. When the meal was finished and the children had exited the lunchroom, Aides collected the items left behind.

The intent of the Department of Agriculture's Food Program was preserved; Lorene was its greatest Champion. She risked her job every day to make sure that leftover, healthy food was consumed by the neighborhood that needed it most.

# 6. JOEY

Joey was a little slip of a boy, almost dainty, but he was all boy. Six years old, his facial features were more chiseled than the other children's. He reminded one of a tiny Frenchman. His mother braided his hair in narrow cornrows, leaving two-inch wisps of braids to frame his face and neck. He was a pretty child; adults, who did not know him, thought he was a girl.

Ms. Grahm was Joey's first grade teacher. In his inner-city public school, the poverty rate was 98%. Federal Agriculture Department breakfasts and lunches, served at school, were often the only food some children ate all week.

By late September, Joey had arrived disheveled and tardy so frequently at school that the Principal sent a District Attendance Officer to his home. Whatever transpired during that visit, Joey's attendance improved. He managed to arrive on time, three out of five days a week; sometimes, he even came to school clean.

Joey walked to school every day with older friends who attended another nearby school. One morning, one of the boys got the bright idea to lob gutter gravel at passing cars. An irate driver leaped out of his car, cornered Joey, and marched him to the Principal's

Office. Joey did a three-day in-school suspension for his bad judgment, his good aim, and his short legs. The 'friends' got away, yet Joey refused to tell on them.

Sometimes Joey was a 'reluctant learner'; Ms. Grahm had to telephone his mom one day to report his uncooperative behavior. His mother came to school immediately, spanked him behind closed doors in the Boys Bathroom, returned him to the classroom, and made him apologize to his teacher and classmates. Standing beside Joey, she promised,

"Joey will do better, because if he don't, I will tear him up again, WORSE! Ain't that right, Joey?" Joey nodded.

He DID do better. He was never going to embarrass his mother again; all Ms. Grahm had to do was threaten to call her on the phone.

One morning he arrived two hours after the first bell. He wore clean clothes, and his hair was twisted into two ponytails like a girl's. The girls pointed and giggled, and the boys whispered as Joey carefully studied the floor.

During the before-lunch bathroom trip, two boys came hurrying down the hallway toward Ms. Grahm.

"Ms. Grahm," they panted, "Joey's 'using it' all over the bathroom!"

"Is it an accident, or is he doing it on purpose?" she asked.

"On purpose!" they chorused. "He made circles on the wall and circles on the floor."

An adult Hall Guard had heard the boys. While he walked toward the two lines of boys and girls, waiting for their turns to use the bathrooms, Ms. Grahm motioned him aside.

He knew Joey. She told him about the girly ponytails and Joey's reaction to his classmates' snickers. She explained that she thought 'peeing' on the floor was a way to assert his masculinity, which the new hairdo totally contradicted. The Guard agreed. He summoned the custodian, under whose supervision Joey would have to mop the floor and wipe down the walls. Joey did so willingly, and when he returned to the classroom, Ms. Grahm said to him, "If I were a boy and my mom had fixed my hair in ponytails, I would probably have to prove that I was definitely a boy, just like you did. But you should not have 'used it' on the floor and the walls. We understand why you did it, but don't ever do it again."

He knew. And he never did do it again.

Sometime later, his baby sister became very ill. Joey

was absent for two days. His mom left a message for the teacher to call her. After they talked about the scare with his little sister, Ms. Grahm told his mom about the ponytails and Joey's bathroom episode. She suggested that Mom consider changing his hairdo for his sake; it obviously upset him to have other children laugh at his hair. She agreed and assured Ms. Grahm she was planning to get his hair cut.

A month passed, and there was no change in the hairdo. Finally, one morning, Joey announced, "Tomorrow is my birthday; I'm getting my hair cut, and my uncle's gonna do it."

The birthday arrived, and so did Joey: in new clothes and freshly-braided cornrows. The cornrows were more intricate than ever before. His classmates sang Happy Birthday to him; Ms. Grahm presented him with a birthday card and a birthday pencil.

But Joey did not come to school the day after his birthday. When the Attendance Officer called his house, Joey's mother hung up on the Officer.

The following day, Joey came to school on time. He was still wearing his new birthday clothes. The fancy 'do' was frazzled and lint-covered, as were the birthday clothes.

"How was your birthday?" Ms. Grahm asked.

"Fine," he answered.

"What happened to the haircut?"

"My uncle said he couldn't do it."

"Did he say why not?"

"Dunno," Joey answered.

"Oh well, I'm glad your birthday was good."

Joey worked exceptionally well that morning, two days after his birthday. He was writing vocabulary words when Ruby raised her hand. Ms. Grahm motioned Ruby to come beside her.

"Joey has a pipe," she said.

The children sitting near him began whispering and holding their noses.

"Oooooo," they complained. "Something smells!" Ruby returned to her seat.

Ms. Grahm motioned for Joey to come. He strolled to the front of the room.

"What have you got, Joey?" his teacher asked quietly.

"Nuthin."

She patted his pants pockets. Inside there was what appeared to be a charred, ragged, plastic cigar holder. Ms. Grahm fished it out and laid it on her palm.

"My momma gave me that, an' she tole me to bring it to school."

"Oh?"

Ms. Grahm had no idea what it was, but from the children's reaction, she suspected it had something to do with street drugs. First-graders are usually pretty truthful, so she called Danisha to step outside the door with her. The doorjamb would hide what was in her hand from the other children's view.

"I dint do nuthin," Danisha whined, as she walked toward the doorway.

"No, you didn't," her teacher said. "I need to ask you something."

They walked to the other side of the doorjamb, and Ms. Grahm held the cigar holder toward her.

"What do they do with this?" she asked.

"They smoke pot and other stuff with those." Her eyes were searching the teacher's.

"Crack?" Ms. Grahm asked.

"Yeah, crack," she said.

"Thanks, Danisha. That's all." Danisha returned to her seat.

The students were getting restless. They had finished their seatwork, but they knew something serious was happening and wanted to hear. The room was silent, except for clanking radiators.

It occurred to Ms. Grahm that Joey was probably asking for help. Earlier that week, she had missed an unspoken plea for help from a hungry dad who had purposely brought his son late to school so he, himself, could get cereal and milk from the kitchen. She realized too late that the dad was hungry too, and she didn't want to make the same mistake with Joey. In regards to the pipe, Joey probably thought that since his teacher had understood the bathroom incident, she could fix this drug problem too.

Ms. Grahm's heart was heavy. She put her arm around Joey and pulled him toward her in a hug. "Does your mom smoke dope with this?" she asked.

"Yeah," he nodded. "She used to jus smoke cigarettes, but now she smokes dope again."

"Do you want her to stop?"

"Yeah."

"Has she ever been to Drug Treatment?"

"She went las year wen I wuz in Kinnergarten." His teacher searched her memory for a solution. "Have you asked her to stop?"

"She don't think I know," he answered. "She goes

out back wi thuh dog."

"I'm SO sorry, Joey. I know you want her to stop. I'll try to think of something."

There was nothing the teacher could do. Drug users who did not obviously neglect their children or abuse them could smoke dope or anything else they wanted in the privacy of their own homes. Ms. Grahm dared not approach Joey's mother herself; his mother would 'tear him up' or her 'dopey' friends would. And he would never dare tell anyone anything again.

If his teacher called County Job and Family Services, someone would come to Joey's home to tell his mother it had been reported that she was doing drugs. She would be warned not to do them and asked if she wanted to return to rehab. This person, usually a high school graduate, earning minimum wage and trained by the County Social Work Department, might as well tell Joey's mother that the 'school had reported her'. How would the school know his mother did drugs at home unless Joey had snitched? There was no way to speak to his mother or anyone else about her drug use without her knowing it was Joey who told on her. To protect Joey, it was prudent to say nothing. Child abuse HAD to be reported to authorities; parents who privately indulged in a drug habit did not.

He had tried to fix his mother, but his trusted teacher, for his own sake, had to let him down(!) The best she could do was to teach him to look out for his own safety.

"Joey, do you have a safe place to go if things get rough at your house?"

"I can go over my cousin's"

"It needs to be someplace really close, Joey, where the person you trust doesn't do drugs or alcohol; someplace where you can run to quickly after dark.

"I trust my grandma; she don't do drugs."

"Would she come get you in the middle of the night?"

"She lives nex door my cousins; she'd come."

"Do you know her phone number?"

"Yeah, I know it."

"If your mom isn't ready to stop, there is not much anyone else can do," Ms. Grahm said sadly. "Can you understand?" "That's the problem with trying to help grown-ups."

His eyes filled. He turned to walk back to his desk.

"Joey, talk this over with your grandma; maybe the two of you can get her to WANT to stop." Joey sat down, put his head down, and hid his face in his arms.

# 7. RONELL

Ronell's first day of first grade was unremarkable. His teacher could not remember anything about him, except that this short, overweight six-year-old boy wore uniform pants which were too big everywhere but his waist.

His pants fell in two puddles of dark blue polyester fabric at his ankles. When he walked, the blue fabric dusted the floor beside him. Luckily for him, he never tripped. Usually, the long pants fell over the top of his shoes and swished to the sides while he walked.

His teacher always knew when he was coming; she could hear his pants.

Ronell's father lived in his own mother's house, and Ronell lived with them. Busing was available to each City School student, but rather than get up earlier to put Ronell on the school bus, his dad chose to drive Ronell to school every morning an hour after school began. From Dad's point of view, at least Ronell was there(!) Every day, promptly at 9 A.M., Ronell stood by the front door, waiting to be let into the school lobby.

*In this district of chronic truancy and abominable graduation rates, a tardy first-grader was considered less than a problem. Principals' yearly raises were, in part, determined by student attendance. Elementary School attendance reports were fudged every day, probably by all the schools.*

One Friday in early October, Ronell arrived late, as usual. His classmates were in the hallway, waiting for their turns to use the bathroom. He had his classroom teacher all to himself that day while an Aid was in the hall with the other children.

"When you get your coat hung up, Ronell, start your 'Bell Work'," his teacher reminded him.

She could hear his pants shuffling toward his desk. His chubby self groaned when he slid into his desk... then silence... and more silence: no desk lid opened, no pencil noises in his pencil tray. She looked up from her Grade Book.

Ronell rubbed his eyes and nose with a wet, grubby little fist. Obviously, he was crying.

"Ronell! What's wrong?" She walked over to stand beside him.

"Here," she handed him some Kleenex.

Ronell stuffed the handful of tissue against his runny nose. "I don like first grade," he moaned. "It's too hard."

He looked beseechingly into his teacher's eyes. "I wanna go back to Kinnergartin." He hiccuped and wiped his nose. "I tole my sister I likt Ms. G, an' she tole me I shuldn't. White people can't be trusted. She's so nice. I love her anyway. I don care whut my sister says." He wiped his eyes and his dripping nose again.

His first grade teacher looked sympathetically at this six-year-old bundle of misery. Maybe he *should* go back to kindergarten. Obviously, he had not mastered last year's skills. He was still guessing at the names and sounds of letters. He wasn't reading because he couldn't sound out words. He didn't like to write because he said it hurt his hand and made him tired; he rarely turned in any homework. His teacher had to sit him in a back corner of the room, away from the pencil sharpener and the sink, because he argued and threatened to fight any child who accidentally bumped him or whose movement made papers blow from his desk.

It took only a mild distraction to disrupt these eighteen fragile learners. Ronell's disruptions were loud and persistent. It was easier to manage the classroom if Ronell were seated in a far corner.

During her morning break, Ronell's teacher approached the Kindergarten teacher, "Ronell was seldom in school last year," Mrs. G confided. "I think there were family problems. He would have a better foundation if he could repeat Kindergarten. I have room for him now."

THAT was what his first grade teacher had hoped to hear.

"Mr. Johnson," she spoke into the phone to his dad, "Ronell is doing poorly in first grade. He didn't learn last year's skills because he was absent so much. He is still behind this year. Mrs. G and I think he could *FLY* through first grade next year, if he could return to Kindergarten *THIS* year. Sometimes little boys need an extra year."

"Mz. Grahm, they ain't nothin wrong with Ronell; you jus GOTTA BE HARD on him. NO, he don need to go back to no Kinnergarden. Like I say, you gotta be HARD on him! Nice talkin to ya." He hung up the phone.

So Ronell stayed in first grade.

Ms. Grahm tried every way to get Mr. Johnson to bring Ronell to school on time; he lost nearly one full day of school each month in the five hours he was late every week.

She walked with Ronell to his dad's car to try to persuade Dad to bring Ronell on time in the mornings. She sent notes home, hoping the grandmother might help. She even telephoned Mr. Johnson many times. Nothing worked.

Ronell's behavior often needed 'adjusting'. He was his own worst enemy during instruction and desk work. Phone calls to Dad at home usually brought instant improvement. Minus signs beside his name on the blackboard, no snack until work was finished, sending him to another classroom to work brought less immediate results, or none at all.

Ronell claimed he would get a "whupping" if Dad got another phone call. These phone calls home involved Ronell (with the teacher standing nearby) telling Dad his transgressions. Apparently, Dad made good on his threats; Ronell's behavior and attitude would improve dramatically for a few hours. Because of his loud, disruptive 'paybacks' for real or imagined wrongs to his person and his inattention to instruction during lessons, different teachers from different disciplines made phone calls home every week. On this particular day, the Librarian called, the Principal called, and Ronell's teacher called. His dad had had enough.

"I already tole you: You gotta be HARD on him!"

Dad hung up on Ms. Grahm. Never again did he speak to her.

Dad continued to pick him up from school every afternoon, but he parked as far from the front entrance as possible. Ronell would disappear into the crowd of 400 milling students and make a beeline to Dad's car. Within seconds, he and Dad were *gone*!

Ronell was an interesting child. He appeared to be raising himself. "Nobody cares," he said sadly. "My daddy goes to th track, an I don see him. He spends all our money there."

His teacher was trying to figure out a way to help him get his homework done at home. "What about your sister?" she asked.

"She's mean," he answered. "She beat up my mom an chased her outa the house."

"That's more than I need to know; I just want you to do your homework. I wondered if she would help you."

"I don like my sister. Wen my daddy axes her to go to the store, she steals." He continued, "She makes me steal too. She has a list, an she tells me what to take. Wen we're done, she gets me a canny bar or whatever I wan, an she keeps th res."

Every day there were serious decisions to be made about children's health and safety in this neighborhood of gangs and drugs. This was another one. How much and to whom should private family information be revealed? How truthful was Ronell's story? It took but a few seconds to decide it was the store owner's responsibility to police his own merchandise, not the teacher's. It was Dad's responsibility to raise his daughter. Ms. Grahm's information was hearsay; she would say nothing.

For a few weeks in February, Dad disappeared. Ronell's mother entered the picture. She brought Ronell to school every morning and picked him up every afternoon. Ronell said they were staying at a shelter. The mother carried a tiny infant in her arms and walked the stairs daily to check with the teacher about Ronell's progress.

For three weeks, Ronell came to school on time. Suddenly, Dad reappeared. Just as suddenly, the other parent disappeared. In no time, Ronell and Dad were back to their old routine.

One afternoon, after lunch and outdoor recess, before math instruction, Ms. Grahm put the children to work on a math puzzle while she wrote a required 'incident report'. Each child was attentively solving a colorful arithmetic problem.

The 'incident' involved a fistfight during lunch.

Lunch Aids were a few neighborhood ladies who were willing to supervise food service and outdoor recess for hundreds of energetic children every school day. Their pay was less than minimum wage. In return, they were permitted to take the students' closed, uneaten Dept. of Agriculture food servings home, including milk and fresh fruit. Most 'neighborhood ladies' neither read nor wrote competently. Thus, teachers were expected to write up the 'incidents' which occurred during the lunch ladies' watch.

The report was finished and Ms. Grahm set it aside.

"Please stack your materials in one corner of your desk and show me you're ready to start math," she smiled.

Everyone pushed crayons and paper to a corner, wriggled their backs straighter in their seats, folded their hands on their desks, and stared at their teacher — everyone except Ronell.

Completely oblivious and hunkered down over his work, Ronell enthusiastically smeared paste on his puzzle paper. His desktop, hands, and wrists were covered with a thick white layer of Elmer's. Dollops of paste stuck to his face, itchy forearms, and dark blue uniform pants. Everywhere he had itched, he had scratched with his gooey hands.

"Ronell! Stop what you are doing and walk to the sink. *Do not touch* anything!" Ronell paused to squint through a sticky eyelid, focusing one eye on his teacher.

"Go wash your hands," she ordered.

Oblivious, Ronell hunkered down again to continue pasting.

Ms. Grahm walked over to his desk. "What did I tell you to do?"

He kept right on pasting. "I'm not done," he muttered. "Besides, I'm stuck."

Warily, his teacher reached for the gooey paper. Touching it gingerly with the tips of two fingers, she dangled the gooey mess toward the steaming radiator behind Ronell. Cautiously, she laid the paper on top. "You're UN-stuck *now*, Ronell." "What did I tell you to do?"

"Nuthin," he mumbled.

"We both know better, don't we?" No answer.

The other children were squirming. Ms. Grahm was losing patience.

"Go wash up."

He sat, staring incredulously at all the paste.

"*GO*! There are soap and paper towels at the sink."

He didn't move.

"Maybe I should call Mrs. Harris," his teacher suggested.

"I doan care," he said.

Ms. Grahm walked toward the intercom.

"I'm GOING. I'm going." He stood up to walk toward the sink.

"You have one minute to get that paste off of you," she threatened. Her finger was raised to push the intercom button.

Ronell turned on the water.

Ms. Grahm returned to his desk to throw out the empty paste jar. She picked up his math book off the floor and pointed to an empty, clean desk beside Ronell's sticky one.

"Sit here; we're going to do math now."

"I ain' doin it," he mumbled. "I wanna paste. I wuz makin that for my daddy."

"SIT!" his teacher ordered.

Reluctantly, he plopped himself into the seat.

His classmates applauded.

"Ms. Grahm, can we do math now?"

With her Principal's permission, the long-suffering Ms. Grahm finally sent the following letter to Ronell's father.

Tuesday, Feb,4

Ronell spends his days refusing to do his work. He balances pencils on his nose. He throws things from his desk to the floor. He daydreams. He erases the same word five times. He rips his paper. He gets up three times to get more paper because he 'messed up'. He breaks his pencil on purpose and spends precious time sharpening it instead of writing with it. He talks to himself while rocking back and forth in his chair. He tattles incessantly. Whenever words offend him, no matter how trivial, he yells and hits.

Ronell is brought to school an hour late every day. He says he feels very sad; he believes that nobody really cares about him.

I have no work from Ronell to indicate he is prepared for second grade.

This is to notify you that Ronell is failing first grade. A copy of this letter has gone to the Principal, and another placed in Ronell's Student Record File.

Sincerely,
Ms. Grahm

The response to this letter was amazing! Dad dropped off a hungry Ronell at 7:50 every morning for the remainder of the school year. Ronell did his writing and practice assignments promptly and without complaining. Most of the time, he paid attention to lessons, proudly raising his hand to give answers. He still did the hitting and shoving 'paybacks' tit for tat, and he rocked and mumbled while he worked, but he made an effort to show that he was learning. He was able to sound out four and five-letter words. He could read smoothly for an early first grade reader. Ronell was a changed child!

*SOMETHING* motivated him. He never explained what happened; Dad still refused to speak or look at the teacher. Mom never returned. Perhaps Dad was right; there was 'nothing wrong' with Ronell.

In spite of his reluctance to write or read, Ronell's brain was actually absorbing much of the first grade curriculum.

He was thinning out as well. His dress code pants still dragged the floor and were frazzled, but they no longer puddle six inches around his shoes anymore. He was definitely taller. His little round face wore a pleasant expression, especially content, while he rocked and mumbled.

His favorite occupation was to just plainly *sit*. His eyes would glaze into a different world than the classroom. While in this state, he never bothered anybody; he never spoke out of turn. In many ways,

Ronell's school career seemed to be improving.

One morning, the following note appeared in Ms. Grahm's school mailbox. It was signed by the Principal;

---

Tuesday, March 29

Ms. Grahm,

It has come to my attention that you were overheard calling a student 'nappy headed nigger'. I came to your defense, of course, but you need to be more careful how you speak to your students.

Mrs. Harris

---

Ms. Grahm was LIVID! *Never* in her entire life had she ever used those words... not ever! They had no place in her vocabulary, no place in her thought process. Worst of all, her Principal *believed* she had said such a thing.

Racial insults were verbal abuse; verbal abuse was cause for dismissal. She took the note to Mrs. Harris.

"I've *never* said this," she said, pointing to the words. "Who on earth told you I did?"

"Grahm, that is what was reported to me. I'm not at liberty to tell you who it was."

An innocent 'Grahm' shook her head, "I can't

believe this!"

On the way back to her classroom, she hatched a plan to find her accuser.

After the usual morning routine; Pledge of Allegiance, African American National Anthem, and *I AM SOMEBODY!* Ms. Grahm sat at the edge of the reading table, facing her seated students. The children knew something unusual was about to take place.

"Devonte, have I ever, this whole year, EVER called you a nappy-headed nigger?"

"No, Ms. Grahm."

"Have you ever heard me call anyone else those names?"

"No, Ms. Grahm."

"Thank you, Devonte."

"Ruby, have I ever called you a nigger? Nappy-headed?"

"No, Ms. Grahm."

"Have you ever heard me call anyone else names like that?"

"No, Ms. Grahm."

Every child in the room had the same answer. She asked them, one by one.

When she got to William, he said, "You said I was

acting bratty once, but you never called me nappy-headed or the *n*-word."

The children agreed.

In the last seat of the farthest row was Ronell. It was his turn to be asked.

"Have I ever called you nappy-headed nigger, Ronell?"

"Yes, Ms. Grahm."

Every child in the room whirled around to face Ronell. In one voice, they chorused, "LIAR!" "She *NEVER* said that," William added.

"She dint say it in class," Ronell backpedaled.

"Where were you?" Ms. Grahm asked, "When you claim I said that?"

"In the bafroom," he answered lamely. He looked down at the floor.

The children began fussing at him. "She never said that in the bathroom." "She never said it anywhere." "*LIAR!*"

"Ronell, look at me," his teacher spoke earnestly and firmly. "I have *never, ever* called you 'nappy-headed' or 'nigger', and you *KNOW it!*"

Crocodile tears began to flow from Ronell's eyes.

When his tears brought no sympathy, he began to

howl.

His classmates groused at him. "Shut up; you know you're a liar." The howling quieted to a sniffle.

And the teacher recalled his family stories about stealing and money wasted at the race track. Were those tales as accurate as his 'nappy-headed nigger' claim? Did he share his family's racial hate? Was this accusation 'payback' for the parent's letter home? How full of hate was this little First Grader?

He was only six. Surely he was repeating words and ideas he heard at home.

One afternoon, about a week after the nappy-headed nigger incident, while the class was doing a writing assignment, he walked to the front of the room to tell his teacher, "I gotta use it, *bad*!" He stood with his legs squeezed together, grasping his crotch.

Ms. Grahm took one look at his contorted face and said, "Go, Ronell. Go *NOW*." (meaning, leave for the bathroom immediately) Ronell promptly did exactly as Ms. Grahm directed.

His facial expression turned to one of relief, while he stood right there and urinated.

"Ms. Grahm," David shouted, "he's peeing on hisself."

The children watched Ronell with interest. "Ooooh! Thas nasty! Why'd ju *DO that*?"

With all that had gone before this incident, his teacher hadn't realized Ronell was SO cognitively immature. He took her at her word, literally.

Some disinfectant and paper towels would clean up the mess, but Ronell would need some dry pants. Ms. Grahm pushed the intercom button.

"We have a bathroom accident," she reported.

"We're out of clothes except for underwear," a voice responded.

"We need Boys' size 10."

"Ok, send him down."

Ronell dripped into the hallway and down the stairs.

Dad was telephoned; as usual, no response.

The following week was significantly uneventful. Ms. Grahm figured another shoe had to drop sometime soon.

It did. It also showed another side of Ronell.

Every day around 10:00, when morning work was finished, the class stopped school work to take a bathroom break, rehydrate with drinks of water, and enjoy a snack of cinnamon graham crackers.

Ronell had not finished his work yet.

"When you are finished, I'll be back with your crackers," Ms. Grahm told him. "You know the routine." Instead of racing to finish, he did another of his 'tit for tats', this time at his teacher.

Out of nowhere, his teacher heard him say accusingly, "The reason I pee on myself is cuz you *never* let me go ta the bafroom."

*So **that** was how he explained the wet pants to his father when he picked up Ronell that day.*

"This whole, entire year, you have **never** asked to 'use it' until last week," she reminded him.

In her mind's eye, she could picture this scenario:

*Ronell, his dad, his sister, and the grandmother are seated around the kitchen table: all listening intently to Ronell's words. "My teachr don like me. She don never let me go to tha bafroom... an she don never let me have snack, an she calls me 'nappy-headed nigger'."*

*What an **awful** white lady that teacher must be! Poor Ronell!*

At the end of the day, Ms. Grahm dropped off the children who rode the bus, and took the others out the front door for dismissal. A determined Ms. Grahm headed for the Principal's office.

"I know who said I called a student 'nappy-headed'," she announced.

"Who?" Mrs. Harris asked.

Ms. Grahm told her the Ronell story.

"That's not who it was," Harris said.

"You're kidding!"

"Honest to God, Grahm!"

"Harris, I didn't say those words or anything like them. I've **never** said that. It hurts my heart to think *YOU* think I would *SAY* such a thing!"

"Grahm, I never said you did."

"That's not what your note sounded like to me."

"If you **promise** not to tell, I guess I can tell you who it was," she said.

"I promise! **WHO,** Harris?"

"It was Jared's foster mother. She swore she was standing outside your room, and she heard you say that."

*Jared was a seriously behavior-disordered child. So serious that he had to be removed from regular classroom education. When he wanted to make other children feel bad, he would call them 'nappy-headed niggers'. She figured the foster mother called Jared the same name in anger and frustration. To hit a child when they misbehaved was 'abuse,' which the foster mother dared not do. Her behavior would be 'reported' by her children and investigated... and she would lose her foster children.*

*Ms. Grahm should have known the words had something to do with Jared. He was the only one she had ever heard say them, but he had been gone for several months now. Why would the foster mother wait until now to play her ace? When Jared's behavior became unmanageable, even in a behavior-disordered classroom, he was finally removed to a residential facility. There would be no more payments for foster care.* **THAT** *would explain the foster mother's attempt to get Ms. Grahm fired. Ms. Grahm could do* **without her** *money too!*

The War Against Poverty knew no boundaries.

Six weeks before school was dismissed for summer vacation, Ms. Grahm was working in her room with the Aid assigned to her group of 'at risk' students. All had done poorly in kindergarten or not attended it. Five students had failed first grade the previous year. Neglect, lead poisoning, and undiagnosed A.D.D. were the usual causes of her children's learning problems. It was hoped another year of structure and physical maturation would help many achieve academic parity with the other seventy-five 'normal' first graders. In great part, the plan actually worked. All but two of Grahm's would go on to second grade.

...........

On the afternoon of Parent Night Conferences, Ms. Grahm and her Senior Citizen Aid, Mrs. Warren, were sorting student work papers to put into each student's folder.

"Think we can finish sorting these papers before I have to pick up the children?" asked Ms. Grahm. Her students were in Music Class.

A rosy-cheeked, panting Ronell arrived at the classroom door. His puffy, down jacket was soaked as he held a grey knit cap in his hand.

"Oh, Hi, Ronell! Glad you're back. What did the doctor say?"

"He gave me a shot." Ronell rubbed his arm.

"Have you had lunch?"

"I got Mac Donald's."

"Well, hang your coat on the back of your chair; I have to go get the others in a few minutes."

Ronell put his coat on the back of his chair seat and sat down. He watched his teachers hurriedly sorting papers. After a few minutes of silence, he asked, "Know what I want for my birthday?"

"No, I didn't know it was your birthday," his teacher answered.

Neither teacher wanted to talk; they wanted to finish the folders before the students returned. Their words with Ronell would be minimal.

"What would you like to have for your birthday?" Mrs. Warren asked lightly.

"I wanna go to a hotel," he announced.

Ms. Grahm shifted into high alert.

"So Room Service can bring you meals, and you can swim in their pool?" she asked. *How much could Ronell know about hotels, she wondered, this child of such poverty?*

"Naw," he answered in a swaggering tone *(so like his father)*, "I want some music too."

"Music?" She waited for him to continue.

"An then I'm gonna get me a white girl."

Both adults' eyes shot wide open. Their bottom jaws dropped.

"Yeah," he confided. "White girls are the bes kind."

*How much dare a teacher say to a six-year-old?*

Mrs. Warren was shaking with laughter.

*Ms. Grahm reflected, how much does a six-year-old*

*know about white girls at a hotel? How much of what I say will be repeated to Daddy? How much of what I DON'T say?*

Cautiously, she said to him, "Ronell, the kind of white girls who hang around hotels really are not the best kind. I'd stay away from them if I were you."

He let that information sink in for a few seconds.

"My daddy says…"

*His teacher was not sure she wanted to hear what Daddy says. For sure, Daddy did not want HER to listen to what Daddy says!*

Ms. Grahm interrupted.

Mrs. Warren was about to roll out of her chair.

*She knew she had to think of something QUICK! To stop this flow of waaay too much information.*

Mrs. Warren was now choking. She reached for a tissue.

"Ronell, would you like some cookies? A drink?" she asked hastily.

Ronell's eyes lit up. Music and girls were replaced with the immediate prospect of cookies and juice.

Fifth-period bell was about to ring.

Mrs. Warren wiped the tears from her eyes.

Ms. Grahm paused. She cocked her head

69

thoughtfully. A half smile crept across her face. "You know, Mrs. Warren," she confided, "If you want to experience WILDLIFE, teach First Grade!"

She fled to the Music Room.

# 8. AYESHA

It was late August on the first day of school. Breakfast had been served, fold-out tables pushed back up into the side walls, and 400 children were seated cross-legged on the Gym floor. Parents congregated around the perimeter. From the stage, the Principal called out teachers' names with the list of students assigned to each room.

"First Grade, Room 212, Ms. Grahm."

Ms. Grahm walked to the front of the Gym. One by one, each child's name was called to line up in front of her. When everybody assembled, Ms. Grahm led her eighteen first-graders and their parents up the back stairs to her first grade classroom.

That day, the children were silent. They watched their new teacher, wondering what would happen next.

The first day of first grade was an important milestone, so important that parents escorted their six-year-olds to school. They stayed for breakfast, they stayed for room assignments, they stayed to meet their child's teacher, and they stayed to make sure their child was 'happy' (translated: the parent was happy with the teacher!). For moms, the first day of first grade was almost as traumatic as the first day of kindergarten.

"Your child's name is printed on the front of a desk. Please find it and help your child get settled. When you have their supplies inside their desks, please put the empty book bags on a hook in the coat closet. I'm coming around to put name tags on the front of each child's uniform so I can learn their names faster. Thank you for all your help this morning. You're welcome to stay if you wish."

Last year's kindergartners happily scrambled into their new 'big kid' first grade desks. Most of them could recognize their name taped to the desk front. When they lifted the desk lid, a box of 24 new Crayolas, a fat pencil with an eraser, real scissors with pointed tips, and a bottle of Elmer glue looked back at them, begging to be tested immediately. Very few parents could supply their children with everything needed. To be sure each child had enough, Ms. Grahm purchased school supplies for each of her students.

"Go ahead, boys and girls. Use your crayons to do the worksheet on your desk. Use whatever you need to make something really nice to take home today."

Moms looked around the room. Every child was busy, contentedly working. One by one, the moms hugged their first graders and congregated by the classroom door.

"Dismissal is at 2:20," Ms. Grahm reminded them. Parents waved another goodbye, which was barely noticed, and they left.

Ms. Grahm knew that this quiet participation was a temporary state of affairs. When these new first graders knew each other and the territory better, their silent, 100% cooperation would be more difficult to gain. In the meantime, their teacher would enjoy every minute of it.

Ms. Grahm stopped at Ayesha's desk, marker poised to write the little girl's name on a self-stick white name tag.

Ayesha's mother had decided to stay.

"I know the right way to spell this name is A-I-E-S-H-A," her mother explained, "But I wanted my baby girl to have a more unusual name, so I decided to spell it A-Y-E-S-H-A."

"Well, hello *AYESHA*," Ms. Grahm smiled and considered it. "That's what it'll be. I'm glad you're here." She wrote the name and stuck the tag on Ayesha's navy blue jumper front. "Here you go."

Ayesha continued to color on the worksheet Ms. Grahm had provided. She seemed comfortable, so her mother walked directly across the hall to second grade to check on Ayesha's brother.

Ayesha was small and thin with cocker spaniel brown eyes. Her hair was pulled back from her face in a single ponytail, and her hairline was framed with short, torn wisps of thin, dark brown frizz. Her navy blue school uniform hung loosely from her narrow shoulders and tiny waist. She appeared small and fragile in her big kid desk. On this first day, she watched her teacher carefully but never spoke.

As the days and weeks progressed, it became obvious that Ayesha enjoyed school, even though she rarely talked. Her greatest wish was to learn to read. She recognized upper and lower case letters of the alphabet, and she memorized the sounds each letter made. She could 'sound out' three and four-letter words.

Ms. Grahm borrowed 50 books every two weeks from the city library and kept them on an open shelf in the classroom. She also got library card applications for everyone. Ayesha pored over the books. Her desk was stuffed with books she had forgotten to return to the shelf.

But, she dreaded handwriting. Every day was a battle to get her to practice it.

"Ayesha, you need to finish this handwriting paper."
Ayesha stared, hands in her lap.

"Ayesha?" Her teacher pointed to the blank lines.

Ayesha looked at them. "Ayesha! Answer me."

Ayesha turned her paper, with its unfinished rows of upper and lower case Ps, face down on her desk.

"Ayesha, we *HAVE* to write, and you have to practice it. Remember your brother last year?"

Silence.

"Ayesha?"

"Uhh."

"What happened at the end of last year because he wouldn't write?"

Silence.

"Ayesha!"

"My mom hadda come to school to *MAKE* him write. He wuz failin."

"Is that what you want to happen to you?"

"No, Ms. Grahm."

"Okay, then," Ms. Grahm turned the paper, *Pp* side up. "Three more lines of *Pp*'s. If they are done well, you won't have to do them anymore. But I promise you, we will do another letter of the alphabet everyday until we practice them all."

Ayesha sighed. She bent over her paper to finish the *Pp's*.

This reluctance to practice handwriting spilled into all writing; spelling words, sentences, and short paragraphs. Luckily, Ayesha wanted to please worse than she wanted not to write. After her initial resistance, she always caved into her teacher's wishes. She knew she would have to practice writing, but it was interesting to see what her teacher would invent to get her to finish her papers. She knew she had written at least a million *Pp's* already. Why should she have to write more? It took five weeks and one day to get through the alphabet *ONE* time; writing took *forever!*

By the end of the year, Ayesha's handwriting was legible; her spelling was at grade level, and she was writing rhymes and notes to Ms. Grahm. She signed them, "I love Ms. Grahm from Ayesha."

Her habit of not speaking caused Ayesha no end of problems. Larger kids ran into her on the playground. Bullies took her dessert at lunchtime. When she needed something, or someone was taking advantage of her, she did not know how to help herself. Instead, she silently stood by, hoping someone would notice the injustice and take care of it *for* her. She never tattled.

"Ayesha, why aren't you working? Where is your pencil?"

Head down, eyes shielded, sitting at the desk across from Ayesha's, Jared wore a smug little smile. He knew where her things were. Most of the time he was using them. It was easier to reach across his desk to hers than to rummage through wrinkled papers, books, and broken crayons to find his own pencil or the color of crayon he wanted.

"*HE* has it," William pointed.

"Ayesha, why didn't you say something?"

Silence.

"Jared, please give Ayesha her pencil. Use your own."

"He can't find it," William interrupted.

"Jared, what is the courteous thing to do?"

"So-rry."

"Jared, say it like you mean it."

"I'm sorry, Ayesha."

"What else do you need to do?"

Silently, he shoved her pencil across his desk to hers.

It was now early October, and Ayesha had had enough of Jared's unasked 'borrowing'. A disgruntled Ayesha raised her hand.

"Yes, Ayesha?"

Ayesha glared at Jared.

"Ayesha, you need to say what is bothering you. Tell me, with words."

"Ms. Grahm, Jared's got my crayons and my pencil."

"You got that right," muttered William.

*Finally!*

"Jared, you have helped yourself to Ayesha's things one too many times. *Actually, the first time was too many.* Find your pencil, get a piece of writing paper, and write ten times, 'I will ask Ayesha's permission to use her supplies'." Ms. Grahm wrote the sentence on the board.

Ms. Grahm continued, "When you have finished the ten sentences, bring the paper to me. Today and every day, you need to use your *own* supplies. *Do not* take someone else's."

Jared slid Ayesha's belongings back to her.

"Thank you, Jared."

...........

Before anyone realized how fast the days were flying, First Quarter Report Cards were due.

"Boys and girls, from 4:00 until 6:00, your parents

will come to pick up report cards today. Your moms want to see how you keep house, how neat your desks are. We want them to like what they see, right?"

"Yes, Ms. Grahm." A chorus of nods accompanied their 'yes'.

"I will help you through a major house cleaning this first time. Are you ready? Heads up, eyes on me, feet on the floor." She looked around the room to be sure she had everyone's attention. She stared intently at anyone not cooperating.

The *LOOK* always brought immediate results.

"Without talking," she continued, "find a tall book inside your desk and prop open the lid with the book." Everyone did as they were told; everyone but Ayesha. She sat staring straight ahead.

"Ayesha, you need to do this too."

"I'll help her, Ms. Grahm," Deonte volunteered.

He rummaged through books and papers until he found a tall library book. He stood it up against her raised desk lid. "Now, without talking, take out all the books and stack them on the floor under your desk." Ayesha didn't move.

Deonte raised his hand again. "I'll help her," he offered. He finished his own, and then fished out all her books and set them under her desk.

She sat.

"Dontcha know how to do nuthin?" Deonte whispered.

"Okay, children. Now collect all your loose papers and throw them into the black trash bag over here. Your best papers are posted on the bulletin boards or are already in your Parent Folders."

Mrs. Warren, the Senior Citizen Classroom Aid, who was sitting at her own first grade desk at the back of the room, watched the cleanup. She said to Ayesha, "Do what your teacher tells you."

Reluctantly, Ayesha stood up. Her uniform was wet. There was a puddle in her chair. She looked confused and pitiful like she didn't know what to do.

"Mrs. Warren, would you please get a roll of paper towels and some soap from my closet and take Ayesha to the bathroom?"

"It's okay, Ayesha, accidents happen. Go with Mrs. Warren."

Ms. Grahm turned to the intercom above her head and pushed the call button. "We have a bathroom accident," she reported. "I need dry clothes for a very small, very wet six-year-old girl."

"Send her down," a voice answered.

Mrs. Warren and Ayesha were no sooner out the door than Ruby shrieked.

"A COCKROACH, Ms. Grahm! Ooooo!" She jumped away from the startled cockroach, which had just landed on the floor.

Sure enough, a three-inch monster with waving antennae and four-inch wings had flown out of Ruby's desk. It was too stunned to run for cover.

Kierra leaped from her seat. She ran to the roach and stomped on it, scraping her shoe back and forth across it.

She stared proudly at the smashed insect carcass on the floor.

"Ain't I good, Ms. Grahm? An I ain't even afraid."

"You're terrific, Kierra! Kierra, the cockroach killer! Thank you."

"Eew!" From a safe distance, the other children peered at the squashed insect remains on the floor. "Nasty!" Just then, there was a knock at the classroom door.

The School Office Clerk was waiting there. With one eye on her students and one eye on the Clerk, Ms. Grahm walked to greet her.

The students sat quietly, interested to hear what was said.

"You're not going to believe this," the clerk said to Ms. Grahm. "We couldn't announce this 'visit', so Harris sent me around to tell everyone. Myers-Moreno is in the building."

"And...?"

"She wants to see how we do Dismissal."

*Myers-Moreno was the new Superintendent of Schools. She often dropped in unannounced to check on her buildings. She was famous for firing Principals on the spot, for dereliction of duty or insubordination if they tried to defend themselves. All personnel sighed enormous sighs of relief when she left a building.*

"She's in Harris' office now."

"Thanks, Carol; we'll be ready."

Carol went across the hall to the second grade room.

*What timing! Desk contents were all over the floor, major housecleaning, a wet child, a dead cockroach, homework to distribute, coats and book bags yet to pack up, no academic learning (as ordered) currently underway, and the Superintendent was on her way upstairs.*

Ms. Grahm shrugged her shoulders. *"One thing at a*

*time," she reminded herself, "You're not allowed to panic."*

*"First things first."*

"I'll take care of the roach," she said. She bent over to wipe it up with Kleenex from her pocket.

Mrs. Warren returned with Ayesha.

"Mrs. Warren, we had an insect invasion while you were gone." Mrs. Warren wrinkled her forehead into a question mark. "Please, would you give this spot on the floor a squirt with the disinfectant? I'll wipe it up in a minute."

In the meantime, Ayesha's mom saw her in the hall and came over to see what was happening.

"Bathroom accident," Ms. Grahm told her. "We didn't know."

"Ayesha, how come you didn't say nuthin?" asked her mom.

Silence.

"Ayesha, do you hear your mom?"

Silence.

"She don't never help herself, Ms. Grahm, an she don't say *nuthin*." Ayesha was looking at the floor; tears gathered in her eyes.

"This is the year she will learn to speak up for

herself, right, Ayesha?"

Ayesha nodded sadly.

"Maybe you would take her with you when you go.
it's almost time for dismissal."

"No, I'll meet her at home; we need to talk, Ayesha."
And her mother walked down the stairs.

Ayesha's shoulders slumped.

"Do you know when you have to use it?" asked Ms.
Grahm.

"Sometimes," Ayesha answered. "An sometimes it
jus comes out."

"Ayesha, I think you need to tell your mother that.
Maybe you need to see a doctor."

*Ayesha was still wet, all the way down to her socks.
The office had only underwear to fit this tiny little girl.
She would have to ride the bus home in obviously wet
clothes. Other children would tease her. Ms. Grahm
couldn't figure out why Ayesha's mother wouldn't let
her walk home with her. Maybe she **wanted** Ayesha to
be embarrassed.*

*Ms. Grahm bent down to wipe up the disinfected
insect juice. A real classroom was nothing like the
textbook classrooms taught at the College of Education.
Who would believe it?*

The following morning, Ayesha's mom brought Ayesha to school. "She won't wet herself no more, Ms. Grahm. We talked about it las night."

"When you have to *go*, Ayesha, just raise your hand and walk out the door. I'll know why you are leaving. Don't even take time to ask." Ms. Grahm smiled.

Ayesha returned the smile.

*Twice, Ayesha got to the bathroom in time. The third time, she didn't make it. And the office still had no extra clothes. Her mother took charge of the dry clothing department.*

"Ms. Grahm, here's extra close for Ayesha to wear." She handed a plastic grocery bag to her daughter. "Put these in your desk," she ordered.

Ayesha walked to her desk and dutifully shoved the bag inside it.

"Thank you, Mrs. Wilson."

*First grade was more successful than Ayesha ever dreamed. Her 'accidents' were rare; she claimed ownership when Jared or anybody else helped themselves to her belongings. She learned to watch for rough play, to move away from it, and she could read.*

*A month or two later,* at the next desk cleanout, Ms. Grahm watched Ayesha hide the plastic bag of clothes inside a pile of raggedy old papers. Furtively, she dropped the pile into a waiting trash bag, stealing a glance at Ms. Grahm.

Did her teacher notice the bag of clothes?

Ms. Grahm looked the other way. Did she notice? Of course not(!)

At the lineup for dismissal, Ms. Grahm put an arm around Ayesha.

"I'm really proud of you, Ayesha. You're writing, you're speaking up for yourself, and you haven't had an accident for two months."

"I know," she said proudly. "I used to be a scaredy cat." She hugged Ms. Grahm.

...........

Ayesha's greatest accomplishment and contribution was yet to occur. It came about in the following way.

*The half-hour before lunch was a perfect time to read aloud to her children. Every school morning for nine months, they worked hard at Language Arts for an hour and a half. A good story was always in order. Ms. Grahm thought of reading out loud to her students as 'Language Personified', one of the main reasons for long and careful Language Arts instruction.*

Maybe someday, one of these students would be

writing books!

"Clear your desks, please. Hands folded on top. Feet flat on the floor."

*Her students loved the Miss Norris books. They described a pretty, young teacher outwitting her students, who were MUCH 'badder' than themselves. The stories were funny and very close to the truth.*

Ms. Grahm pulled out her chair and sat down. She looked around at her students. Quiet anticipation registered on every face,

Miss Norris Has a Sports Day
Written by Mary Alloway
Illustrated by Jimmie Jones

*For some weeks now, gloom had blanketed the Alan J. Duncy School.*

*No one smiled or giggled.*

*No one even spoke.*

*Miss Norris was worried.*

Ayesha couldn't stand the suspense. She wanted to see the illustrations. She loved being read to. She loved these stories. Quietly, she left her desk. She walked to the front of the room, beside Ms. Grahm reading, and put an arm around her teacher's shoulder, better to see the illustrations. Ms. Grahm kept right on reading.

*Everyone was discouraged.*

*Even the cooks forgot their favorite recipes.*

*Mr. Dullard was so discouraged, he hid in his closet.*

*"It's the worst soccer team in the whole city," he said.*

When Ms. Grahm didn't stop Ayesha, William left his desk too. Silently he sat on the floor, facing the still-reading Ms. Grahm.

*And it was true — the Alan J Duncy Dangers were positively pathetic.*

*They had never won a game!*

One by one, all eighteen children left their desks to sit close to their teacher while she read to them. Not one disagreement, not a single shoving incident, not a word.

Ms. Grahm held up the book so everyone could see the pictures.

She continued reading.

For twenty minutes, this class of 'at risk' first graders sat engrossed, listening to the story. Ms. Grahm was amazed.

The next day, the same thing. One by one, as instinctively as language is instinctive, the children were drawn to a good story.

Until the very last book on the very last day of first

grade, these children of extreme poverty gathered quietly around their teacher's chair to listen and to learn and to be entertained.

*"Language is POWER," she thought to herself.*

*Miss Norris went home from school weary and happy.*

# 9. DISAPPEARING ACT

*BOOM!* The building shuddered; the Boiler Room windows blew out. Dusty smoke poured into the late October air. The explosion was so loud the sound of shattering windows went unheard.

It was the 'first lunch' period. Most teachers ate in the Teacher Lounge, and students ate in the Gym. Ms. Grahm ate at her desk.

As soon as she felt the noise, Ms. Grahm knew exactly what had happened. She ran to her classroom windows to look down at the Boiler Room roof. It was intact. Most likely, only one of the two boilers had blown. Her students were in the Gym, as far from the classroom as they could possibly be, and still be inside the building. She needed to get them out of harm's way. She flew down the stairs and ran to the far end of the main hall. Teachers were gathered in the hallway, talking about the noise. She hurried past them.

At the Principal's office, she stopped to tell Mrs. Harris what she had observed.

"I already know, Grahm. We can't evacuate until I have the okay from Downtown. I'm waiting for a return call now."

"The Boiler Room could blow up that section of the

building, classrooms with kids, and you have to wait for *permission* to evacuate from Downtown?"

"That's the way it is, Grahm."

Grahm left, headed for the Gym. She could hear Harris' phone ringing in the background. Her children stood when she arrived at their lunch table. She lined them up and marched them outside, away from the building. If these were her own children, she hoped their teacher would have the courage to do the best thing for their sake. If the District gave her a hard time for doing what she knew was right, she, the Teachers' Union, and her million-dollar insurance policy would pay for her lawyers.

The emergency sirens screamed on Fifth Avenue, but none stopped at the school. Many minutes later, other teachers with their students also came pouring out of the building to line up in the relative safety of the parking lot.

Ms. Grahm had stopped her group on the sidewalk beside the school fence, as far from the building as possible.

Black cars of Official District Security began to pull into the school parking area near the boiler room. Men in dark business suits hurried out of their cars. The school fire alarm blasted its four on/four off rhythm. Shivering and talkative, her students were curious, but not afraid.

"This is a real one," their teacher told them. "I think there was a fire in the Boiler Room. We'll wait here until they tell us it's safe to go back inside."

Fire drill evacuations were mandated practice each month. To wait quietly for an 'ALL CLEAR' buzzer was nothing new to these children.

In her mind, while everyone was waiting, Ms. Grahm recalled her arrival earlier that morning. At 7 AM, it was still dark, and she could see her breath in the cold air. Alone in the parking lot, she entered through the Custodian's door at the Boiler Room because it was closer, hopefully safer, than the school's rear entrance. A new Custodian, whose breath reeked of alcohol, greeted her on the concrete walkway above the school's enormous boilers.

The antique boilers glistened with coats of bright, candy-blue enamel paint. This new Custodian/Boiler Operator's chief responsibility was the safe operation of the school's heating system. Every other duty was secondary. No one was permitted to be a Custodian without a Boiler Operator's license. His office was directly adjacent to the Custodian Entrance door; his official certificate hung on the wall. Briefly, he and Ms. Grahm commented about the pervading smell of hot metal and fuel oil fumes.

She opened the Boiler Room fire safety door into the main hallway, where the air looked clear but smelled heavily like the Boiler Room. The odor was less pungent upstairs in her classroom, but she could feel a headache coming on.

The morning had proceeded like all other late October mornings; radiators clanking, valves hissing, cold wind blowing through leaky windows, while first graders learned the basic patterns of their English language. According to the new Custodian, there was no sign of anything wrong with the steam boilers.

The ear-splitting, insistent, 'ALL CLEAR' buzzer called her back to the present, chilly reality. Her little ones were shivering. She raised one hand above her head. The rule was to close your mouth while an adult's hand was raised. The children copied their teacher's lead.

"I know you're cold," she sympathized. "*Without running*, without acting silly, we will walk back into the building. We can talk about this when we get into the room."

Ms. Grahm walked to the front of their line, put her hand down, faced the students, and walked back up to Room 212. Excited ADHD children had a hard time controlling impulsive behavior. To be sure *all* her students were on their best behavior while they walked back to their room, she watched them while they walked. No one liked *THE DREADED LOOK!*

For many reasons, not the least of which was the bathroom, they needed to get inside quickly.

The remainder of this shortened afternoon sped past uneventfully. After dismissal, she returned to the Principal's Office.

"I know you took your kids outside, Grahm, and you were right," Mrs. Harris told her.

"I'm glad you agree with my decision; I was worried. What happened, Harris?"

"The smell was getting worse down here, so I sent the Custodian again to check on the boilers. He said he climbed all over them, looking for problems. He read the gauges and returned to me to report that nothing was amiss. He had no sooner walked out my door than the boiler exploded. There's a six-foot deep hole blown out of the concrete and the dirt underneath it."

"Oh my god! Harris. What if the boiler had exploded from the top?"

"I don't even want to think about it."

*400 children, 25 teachers, 15 adjunct staff were in the building every school day.*

The following morning, a new custodian greeted the arriving teachers. Noise from the only working boiler was deafening. As if nothing had ever happened, 'Downtown' managed to maintain total silence; no talk, no news, no emergency vehicles, no notes home.

***WHAT*** explosion?

# 10. MAURICE

It was cold and rainy outside, a typical November morning. The school room was warm and bright; radiators clanked, and fluorescent lighting glowed while children worked quietly at their desks. Ms. Grahm was at a corner table, directing a six-year-olds reading group. Unnoticed, a small boy dressed in a red ski jacket, accompanied by a woman in a dripping wet, floor-length brown coat, appeared silently in the doorway.

Ms. Grahm looked up from the reading group.

"If he gives you any trouble, call me," the woman announced.

The teacher stood up to greet them, but the speaker had already disappeared as quietly as she had come. The boy held out a District Transfer Form toward Ms. Grahm.

*The sight of this small, anxious child in the long red jacket made her sad, but worse was the adult who seemed so eager to abandon him. For an instant, she felt a surge of anger toward the woman, and sympathy for the little boy.*

*Who drops off a first grade child to fend for himself alone in a new room, in a new school, with new kids and a new teacher? But she pushed those thoughts out of her mind to make room for her best smile, careful to speak to him cheerfully. She wanted him to feel welcome.*

"Hi! Welcome to Robeson! My name is Ms. Grahm; what is your name?"

The boy answered softly, "Maurice."

"Boys and girls, this is Maurice."

"Ms. Grahm, Ms. Grahm, can he sit by me? I can show him everything."

"Andrew, you are the man of the hour."

"What's that mean, Ms. Grahm?"

"It means you are the man for the job. It means 'yes'." Andrew grinned.

"Maurice, this is Andrew; Andrew, this is Maurice."

Maurice looked anxious, but he seemed pleased with Andrew's willingness to be his guide on this first day in a new school. The red jacket he wore was so oversized it hung to his knees. He had no book bag and no school supplies.

*Perhaps the red jacket was his mother's jacket, which was why the woman who brought him was wearing the floor-length coat. Was that woman his mother? Who knew?*

*There were large, deep scars on Maurice's left*

cheek and left forehead. One couldn't be sure how kids got the scars, but you knew to keep an eye on their arms and shoulders; legs too, if you could...just in case.

"Andrew, would you please show Maurice the coat closet and find an empty hook for his jacket?"

"While you are doing that, I'll get him pencils and crayons. For right now, the two of you can share your books; I'll get him his own while you are at lunch."

The Transfer Form gave Maurice's age as eight years. He was a first grade repeater from his previous school. He sat quietly beside Andrew, carefully copying everything Andrew did. He waited for Andrew to start writing, then copied whatever he wrote. All morning they sat together.

Two weeks later, cooperative, shy Maurice's honeymoon with the new school ended. By his second day in her classroom, Ms. Grahm realized he could not read. He had copied Andrew's writing but had no idea what it said. As more school days passed, more holes in his learning became evident, as did his attempts to disguise them.

He didn't know the names of alphabet letters, and he didn't know their sounds. He couldn't write; he *drew* the letters. He didn't know how to count, nor did he know the correspondence between numbers and their numerical value. He knew nothing about money.

*So what does an eight-year-old boy, who has already spent two years in the first grade, **do** in yet another first grade room to avoid drawing attention to his academic failures?*

He started complaining that other boys were 'messing' with him; Ms. Grahm watched diligently. She observed him *start* the 'messing' by quietly calling names, threatening to fight with boys who sat near him or passed his desk, and when the boys retaliated, he complained *they* were messing with him.

*First answer to all the above questions; Maurice started the 'messing'. He bullied them, and fear of his size removed their urge to insult him.*

The children in Room 212 did not like Maurice; they were afraid of him. He was taller, his face was scarred, and his clothes were large and dirty. For many weeks he was 'that new boy'. They never called him by his name, just 'new boy', BUT he showed them he could draw, which they respected.

Second answer to the above question; he could draw better than they could, and he gladly made them gifts of his drawing if they asked. A carefully drawn picture of

Mega Taurus One was his bartering tool; it bought him unquestioning admiration.

Maurice had not hit anyone yet. He had not been in any fights but was ready to explode; all he needed was the right spark. He did NOT like school, understandably. All he wanted to do at school was to draw. Drawing was successful.

When Ms. Grahm would correct him publicly for his insulting words or uncooperative behaviors, he would stare into her face, open his eyelids as wide as they would stretch, keep them open, and roll his eyeballs toward the back of his head. This was a way children in this neighborhood showed disrespect. Done to a peer, it was a provocation for a fight; done to an adult, it was a symbol of deliberate insolence.

"Maurice, when you roll your eyes like that, you look like the Village Idiot."

*She hesitated to use the word 'idiot', but she needed to make him look and feel silly enough, embarrassed enough, to stop the behavior.*

Her students tittered cautiously. They too, had been known to roll their eyes when they didn't like what was said to them.

"If you want to look like an idiot, that is your choice,

but you really do look silly." He was convinced!

The behavior stopped.

Maurice **loved** to draw more than anything in the world. He could draw the *Mega Taurus One character* to look exactly like it looked in comic books and on TV. He drew this figure over and over.

Jared, also a repeater, and probably the angriest, most unstable child in the room, was particularly impressed. In *his* mind, no one could draw like Maurice could. Jared never challenged Maurice.

When it was time to begin a lesson during instructional time, Ms. Grahm would say to the class, "Take out your books now, and turn to page…"

*Not Maurice; he would keep right on drawing.*

"Please clear your desks," she would repeat in a no-nonsense tone while *staring directly at Maurice with THE LOOK.*

Maurice would continue to draw or, worse, get up out of his seat to get another piece of paper from the paper table.

No *kindly* tactic convinced him to stop drawing. He tuned out his teacher' directions.

*Was this passive, or active aggression? Did it really matter? He needed to learn what she was teaching.*

When she walked to his desk to remove the offending paper, she removed it gently so as not to tear it, but when she marched toward him not-so-kindly, he could hear her coming *LOUD* and *CLEAR*. Instantly, he shoved the drawing inside his desk.

When he *concentrated*, he could *remember* a few letters and the sound each letter made. The trick was to force him to *focus*. Praise and encouragement kept him motivated once he got started. His progress moved at a snail's pace, but it was far more than he had accomplished during his other first grade placements. She was hopeful.

One day, the Principal mentioned, in an offhand way, that Maurice had been expelled from his previous school.

*Grahm remembered his first day at Robeson. Maybe **that** was why the woman had dropped him off so abruptly. It was **his** fault she had to leave home to walk in the rain to enroll him in a new school. She was NOT happy with Maurice.*

*But what on earth does a first grader do to earn expulsion?*

"That's what I heard at the Principals' meeting," Mrs. Harris explained.

Maurice's progress in Language Arts was worse than slow. He had an awful time remembering letter sounds: he would remember them one day; forget them the next. He SO wanted to draw instead.

Many was the piece of noncompliant artwork she had to throw out to convince him he HAD to learn the assigned letters and sounds *first*. When he accomplished *that*, THEN he could draw.

*And one thing about Ms. Grahm was, she kept her word! You could ask anyone.*

He and Ms. Grahm struggled mightily, but *she* stayed at it, and by January, he could remember, he could sound out, even *read*, a few three-letter words.

*"Nothing succeeds like success!" she congratulated herself.*

But one Monday morning, Maurice appeared in adult-sized women's slacks and a woman's shirt at school. He wore them all week. Every cuff had to be rolled up four or five times to use his feet and hands. Sometimes he stuffed the too-long pants into his shoes. His classmates did not make fun of him, but Ms. Grahm was concerned.

Would the too-large, colorful, grown women's clothes interfere with learning? She tried to telephone his mother, who could not be reached because a 'disconnected' phone number had been given on the day he was registered.

Other students from other rooms *did* insult him; it was only a matter of time before he stopped them with fists.

Now into the second week of the recycled women's fashions, Maurice and the other students in his class were waiting outside the bathrooms to take turns using it. They stood quietly in two lines; boys and girls.

The too-large waist band of Maurice's pants was held up by an adult-sized belt into which a hole had been punched to accommodate his eight-year-old waist. The end of the belt hung an extra twelve inches front and center, usually hidden by one of the knee-length shirts he always wore.

Bored, standing quietly in line, it wasn't long before Maurice realized what a high old time he could have with that belt piece. When he thought Ms. Grahm wasn't looking, much to the girls' dismay and the boys' delight, he gleefully brandished the twelve-inch hanging plastic strap as if it were a very long piece of his private anatomy. He swung it to the left; he swung it to the right; he spun it around in concentric circles while the girls squealed and the boys whooped. He grinned mischievously throughout the exhibition.

*The whole thing was too funny; what spunk this little guy had!*

But Grahm couldn't let it continue. What would the girls tell their mothers? The boys, of course, thoroughly enjoyed the whole show.

"MAURICE!"

Fixing her sternest glare in his direction, he wilted.

"Do you want to hold up those pants with a string tied in the belt loops, or do you want to keep the belt? If I EVER see that again, you KNOW what I'll do!"

He knew.

His clothing situation was bad for many reasons. Grahm was pleased that he could make fun of it with the belt arrangement, but it was time to give Maurice some help with hygiene and a wardrobe.

Obviously, he did not have any dress code clothing. In the beginning, he wore blue pants and colored long-sleeved shirts – sometimes a white one – but they were not the standard uniform the District required. His were obviously way too large.

So one afternoon, deliberately walking with him at dismissal time, she studied him carefully. His body was dirty, his teeth full of cavities, and his shoes were too small. Over his ill-fitting clothes, he wore the now grimy jacket, which used to be red.

"Maurice, would you like to have 'dress code' to wear to school?"

He brightened. "I'd like that," he said.

"I'll see if I can get you some," she promised. "You run along home; I'll see you tomorrow." VERY softly, he said, "Ms. Grahm, I love you." And he ran down the sidewalk.

A young woman Ms. Grahm didn't know approached her.

"Is he giving you any trouble?" she asked.

"We're just talking," Ms. Grahm answered. "Why do you ask?"

"I have two daughters in school here." She described her girls' accomplishments, adding that she sometimes drove Maurice home to help out his mother. Shielding her mouth with a cupped hand, she said quietly, "His mother has five children under the age of eight. Maurice is the oldest. She's twenty-two years old."

Ms. Grahm was stunned. It took a few seconds for her to catch her breath. She did the math. Poor Maurice!

"When you talk to his mother, tell her the school will

get him some things he needs."

The 'school' was not going to 'get' Maurice anything; Ms. Grahm was, but no one needed to know that.

"That would help a lot," the woman answered.

Promptly at 3:00, Ms. Grahm drove straight to the nearest Kmart. An hour later, she returned home with two pairs of navy dress pants, four white shirts, underwear, socks, a pair of shoes, a navy sweater, and a winter jacket. She bought a toothbrush, toothpaste, washcloths, two bars of soap, and a laundry bag. She would teach him how to wash his clothes in the bathtub if his mother did not do laundry.

Driving to school the next morning, she realized that today was one of those days with no planning period. She would not be able to leave the classroom to help Maurice try on the new clothes. Before he took them home, she needed to know if they fit; he *had* to try them on. Who would help Maurice with the clothes and could also be trusted to keep quiet about from whom and where he got the clothes?

There was so much gossip among the help staff, she couldn't think of anyone who fit the requirements she needed.

At school, she went directly to her classroom to lock up the bags of new clothing. Later, on her way to the office to sign in, a Security Guard met her in the main hallway.

"Aha!" She's the perfect person; she won't **talk,** and if she can, she'll be glad to help. Officer Sabo was warm and courteous to everyone; Ms. Grahm liked her. There were Security Officers, and then there were Officers like Sabo.

"I'll be free at 9:15," Sabo offered. "I'll come get him then."

True to her word, Officer Sabo was standing in the doorway at 9:15. She was short and chubby, with short curly hair and brown eyes. She wore a navy uniform with a Walkie Talkie tucked in her belt, which chattered incessantly.

"I came to get Maurice," she said.

Maurice was smiling ear to ear.

"The bags are right here," Ms. Grahm pointed.

Maurice grabbed them all.

"Let's go, fella," said Officer Sabo.

A half-hour later, they returned. Maurice was proudly wearing his new shoes, socks, and a dress code shirt.

"The pants are too big; he needs a size 8. 10-12s are too large."

"I'll take them back tonight," Ms. Grahm told Maurice. "And get you the right size."

He turned his back to the rows of seated students and whispered to his teacher, "Ms. Grahm, please, can I have a book bag too?" His dark eyes were unsure and pleading.

Of course, he could have a book bag. She would fill it with everything an eight-year-old first-grader needed: a ruler, some nice pencils, an eraser, scissors, some glue, and some tape. Maybe even a little candy.

"You bet I'll get you a book bag," she answered.

"Send him down tomorrow," Officer Sabo said. "We'll try on the smaller pants."

"Maurice, you look really good in your new clothes!" Ms. Grahm bragged. "How do you feel?"

"I feel good, Ms. Grahm," he answered. He was smiling.

"What do you think, class?"

"He looks good, Ms. Grahm!"

He did look good. She was pleased.

"Cha-ching!" she rang a pretend cash register. "This is going to be a GOOD day! Right, Maurice?"

"Right, Ms. Grahm."

For the next six months, Maurice and Ms. Grahm struggled with his reluctance to learn the first grade curriculum. She was bound and determined he would complete first grade successfully this year. Maurice humored her by doing just enough to earn drawing time. He was bound and determined to perfect every Mega Taurus One figure in the series. Academics, especially language, were a necessary evil to be endured, not to be pursued. Reading and writing were too difficult, and math was okay, but his artistic efforts were, by far, the most important endeavor of his life.

When all was said and done, Maurice did not pass the required State Tests at the end of the year. He still couldn't read well enough to follow written directions, nor could he focus long enough to mark correct answers to questions he could barely read. Like too many children, he marked any old answer to get rid of the test. "See, Ms. Grahm? I'm finished." He needed at least six more months of short, daily reading lessons, and he needed to practice his reading. But there would not be another six months; there would not even be Summer School for him to catch up. Summer school this year had been canceled 'due to budget constraints'.

Maurice, because of his age, would automatically be assigned to second grade next year. He – who was still learning kindergarten and first grade skills – would now be forced to build second grade skills on first grade skills he had never mastered.

Suppose she tallied the District's students, who, like Maurice, could not remember letter sounds, who could not memorize whole words, and whose every class subject required some level of reading which they couldn't do. In that case, she could explain the District's absentee rate, dropout rate, and its extremely small percentage of high school graduates. By age 10, most of these discouraged learners had dropped out of school, even though they occupied desk space in a classroom. Grahm suspected lead poisoning from their pregnant mamas — to the fetus in utero, throughout childhood, and into adulthood — at levels much lower but equally as poisonous (or worse) than those presently set by 'government standards'. Someday, 'acceptable' lead levels would be lowered; she hoped the medical profession would initiate it SOON.

Short of taking them all home with her to raise, she could see no solution in sight. Inner-city's children of poverty were treated like 'throwaways'.

Should Maurice stay at Robeson, Ms. Grahm had his second grade teacher already picked out. This teacher would pick up where Grahm had left off. Success and time were on Maurice's side, even though the School District was not. 'No Child Left Behind'.

Yeah, right!

Maybe the city ought to replace its thousands of miles of hundred-year-old, LEAD water pipes. Kool-aid, coffee, and tea made from city water were responsible for more deaths than any weapon in the hood.

# 11. KING

King was a tall, handsome boy. The children liked him. He rarely spoke. He couldn't read, and he couldn't write. He failed kindergarten the year before, but the District had a policy of promoting all Kindergartners, so he was placed in Ms. Grahm's First Grade class of 'at risk' learners. His mother had transferred him to Robeson this year, hoping last year's teacher was the problem, not her child. The Reading Coach and Ms. Grahm worked diligently with King, but unlike Maurice, King sat quietly in his chair as if he were disconnected from the reality of the classroom. He 'watched'; he didn't participate. He seemed to be 'zoned out'.

Never once, the entire year, could he answer questions about what was being said or about the material being studied. His standard answer was, "I don't know," accompanied by a shrug of the shoulders. When pressed further to answer, his reply was the same, "I don't know."

He showed little interest or emotion in anything but recess. Outside, he played enthusiastically, usually running aimlessly and happily. When the whole group informally played Tag, he was frequently one of the first ones 'tagged'. He never did figure out how to 'tag' someone else when he was 'it'. Everyone, even chubby Ronell, always managed to outrun or outmaneuver him.

Unlike most of the children who finally figured out the formula for reading, King never 'got it'. At the end of the year, he seemed to be as far behind as he was on the first day of school. He sat quietly in his seat, never disturbing others.

Four times a day, five days per week, for ten months, each time he needed to 'head' a paper for a different class, he had to refer to the example Ms. Grahm had permanently written on the chalkboard. He couldn't remember how to do it. His writing was large and scrawly. It took him ten minutes to write his name, the date, and the subject title. When he could, he copied his neighbor's work. He couldn't read what he was writing; he seldom completed writing assignments, but *even a little* writing indicated he knew *something* much more acceptable to himself than an empty paper.

By mid-November, Ms. Grahm realized King's learning disabilities were deeper than simple inattention or failure to grasp kindergarten skills. Whatever was wrong, was severe. In answer to Grahm's request for psychological evaluation, the psychologist assigned to

Robeson told her that she "couldn't get to him this year, but would put him on the list for next year." The District expected this one psychologist to service a 1400-student Middle school four days/week and the 400-student elementary school one day/week.

King's mother stopped to sign the testing permission papers on her way to work. It was the first time she had been to the school. She looked very young, with a bright red, two-inch high spiked haircut. She wore heavy makeup and had a gold front tooth. Her looks were startling in four-inch black heels and tight black capris, topped with a tight, black, long-sleeved, scoop neck tee shirt. *NEVER* would Grahm have guessed that she was the mother of the tall, quiet King.

King stayed in Ms. Grahm's room for the remainder of the year. Coach, and she tried *EVERYTHING*; they didn't give up, but King never moved off square one. When Grahm complained sadly to Mrs. Harris about King's lack of progress and her inability to 'fix it', the Principal tried to make both of them feel better.

"You know, Grahm, we can't win them all; some of our kids are just too damaged. We have to accept that."

*Sadly, they both knew she was right.*

# 12. WIRED

Still feeling lethargic from too much Thanksgiving, students and teachers returned from vacation to be met by rising clouds of dust and screaming electrical saws. Stepladders and stacks of eight-foot metal conduit were placed in every corner. Bundles of colored wiring dangled from gaping holes overhead. Sheetrock and wall-board scraps littered the floors. Snow-covered children carrying book bags, and workmen with tools in hand, danced a sidestep around opened ladders to enter classroom doorways. Clean, quiet halls were a thing of the past.

Even the resident cockroach population took cover. Not one poked a head out of its hideout behind the decorative tiles on the hallway walls. On this first day back, construction noise pounded and screeched through The Pledge of Allegiance, Morning Announcements, Bathroom Runs, and ninety minutes of Language Arts. It continued through Lunch, Recess and Afternoon Classes. It accompanied students walking to dismissal in the gym, and finished up at 4 P.M. with a tattoo of staple gun pops.

Ms. Grahm gave a sigh of relief. Finally, the place was quiet. She stayed late every afternoon to prepare her classroom for the next day's lessons. The noise and the dust were unwelcome visitors. She hoped they would be gone soon, but the hanging wires, the unused conduit, and the many ladders all indicated an extended stay.

However, her first-graders *loved* the construction mess. They scuffed their shoes in the dust to draw pictures on the floor. They crawled up bundles of metal conduit to hear it ring when it moved around on the piles. They clambered up ladders to peer curiously into unknown recesses above the ceiling. For them, this work site was a playground: a really neat place to explore, at least when grown-ups weren't watching. Grown-ups ALWAYS chased kids off fun stuff, claiming 'someone would get hurt'. Besides, they didn't know anything; they only *thought* they did!

Ms. Grahm had not forgotten her own childhood experiments with water in the kitchen sink and outdoor hose nozzles, with secret fires in a makeshift clubhouse, and walking blindfolded on rafters. But now she was the enemy, a responsible adult. By personal commitment, she harbored a deep respect for childhood experiences, but, by that and by law, she could not allow her first-graders to walk unsupervised so close to such adventurous temptation. Unexpected bathroom trips would now need to be chaperoned.

On day two of the overhead construction, Ms. Grahm wondered how much longer she would have to teach above the noise and the dust. Even through closed doors, it was disturbing.

She decided to approach a workman.

"What are you all doing up there in the ceiling?"

"We're installing new lines for the computers," he answered.

"Doesn't the dust bother you?"

"We're used to it. We do this for a living."

"Oh," she grimaced. "How much longer will you be drilling?"

"Until we're done."

(*You asked for **that**, Grahm!*)

"What about asbestos in these old buildings?"

"There isn't any," he answered. "It's in our contract."

By the third day of dust and screaming tools, of conduit rolling out of corners, of constantly interrupted lessons, every teacher in the building was complaining. The Principal seemed to know as little about the construction as her teachers.

"Mr. Richmond assures me it will all be over in a

few days," she told them.

*Mr. Richmond was the Principal's immediate supervisor, an 'Area Superintendent', newly appointed to a lucrative, newly invented job title, by a newly hired CEO. Previously, he was a ready-to-retire Principal of a large elementary school across town.*

Dissatisfied with their Principal's answer, the teachers silently raised their eyebrows, meeting each others' eyes to express their displeasure.

"That's all I know," Mrs. Harris apologized.

The teachers dispersed.

By day four, Mrs. Phelps, across the hall, was diagnosed with pneumonia. The Special Ed teacher developed severe asthma attacks daily and had to leave early almost every afternoon. Her students were then temporarily sent to other classrooms; Ms. Grahm always received at least one. The School Attendance Report showed teacher and student absence on the rise.

When the children had left at the end of this fourth day, Ms. Grahm watched a workman, clinging to the sides of a ladder, fall down from the ceiling, collapsing in a heap at the bottom. Other workmen rallied around him, sitting him upright on the floor, to spray an asthma inhaler near his mouth and nose until he could catch his breath again. He left the job site on a stretcher, and he never returned.

His collapse represented everyone's unspoken fears about this extremely dusty, hazardous construction project. SOMEONE needed to DO something! Every school in the district was contracted to have new computer wiring installed; Robeson Elementary was one of the first.

Ms. Grahm was seated at her dusty desk on a dusty chair, looking up tomorrow's lesson plans in a dusty Lesson Plan book on a dusty desktop. When she reached for a Kleenex to wipe her runny nose, she realized that even she; her clothes, her hair, her skin, her *nose, and probably her lungs,* were just as dusty.

*None of the workers wore masks, and no one sprayed the dust on the floors or swept it up as it accumulated. There were no exhaust fans to suck dirty air outside. Hired cleaners scoured sinks and swept classrooms at night, but no one dusted unless a teacher did. To Grahm's knowledge, no Company Supervisor ever came around to check on this work site. Unprotected; staff, workers, and students inhaled excessive amounts of dust, soot, and plaster particles. Eight hours a day. EVERY DAY!*

For Grahm, the construction was further complicated by the probability of asbestos contamination. Its use in building materials had only recently been declared illegal. Inhaled asbestos particles over periods of time could be deadly.

While she washed blackboards and wiped out chalk trays, she thought carefully about this problem. Something meaningful needed to be said, and something even more meaningful needed to be done to correct it. But who would do it?

*No one she could think of. The Principal, whose job description included the health and safety of her staff and students, had apparently surrendered that responsibility to her boss. Teachers complained constantly and bitterly to each other, about students, about administration, about building conditions, about policy, especially about this latest construction project, but the bottom line was that gossip and complaints were as far as they intended to take their dissatisfaction.*

*Grahm was older; she never felt like she quite belonged (nor did she want to). Her life experiences had been much different from any of theirs. She wasn't afraid to say what needed to be said, except that it had to be said truthfully and compassionately, directly to the person who needed to hear it. She knew her fellow teachers respected her, even trusted her. They came to her with problems about health, about children, and about husbands. She babysat their disruptive students daily. Grahm knew she held a unique position in the school community.*

*And so did her immediate boss, Mrs. Harris, the Principal.*

So Grahm said to herself, "Who could do this better than you, Ms. Grahm?"

She knew she was at least as smart, if not smarter, than the District's Administrators; not as cunning or devious, but definitely endowed with intelligence, integrity, and respect for life. The use of political correctness – so important to political appointees — was about as high on her list of priorities as were the politically appointed 'administrators'.

So who would fix the breathing problems?

She already knew the answer, and she would give it her best try. Job security might be at stake, but she was due for retirement at the end of this school year anyway. She wasn't much afraid. If she didn't at least try, nothing would be done; no one else dared. Besides, **anyone**, who would deliberately sicken employees and children OUGHT to be exposed and stopped. She had no problem making that happen.

She would wage a quiet, firm, intelligent(!) COLD WAR. The lesser time the innocent civilians were contaminated, the less severe the impact would be on their lungs. Political Entities and Corporations were notoriously speedy to spend their taxpayer millions; she would need to move swiftly and firmly.

So first on Grahm's Cold War Agenda was a trip to her Principal's office.

"C'mon in, Grahm, I've been expecting you. Sit down."

Grahm pulled up an aging, blond, wooden teacher chair. She rested her elbows on the edge of Harris' desk.

"You know, Harris," she said with a straight face, "the mice and the rats hired moving vans yesterday and left."

"Really?" Harris halfway smiled.

"Across the street," said Grahm, without a smile, "where they can breathe."

"You've got *that* right," Harris agreed.

Grahm continued, "I used to date a Mr. FixIt; he worked for years in the construction trades. These old buildings are full of asbestos; no one wanted a school to burn down, and at that time, asbestos was legal. I don't believe, for one minute, that there is *no* asbestos in this building or that we're not breathing it. Its effects are cumulative; I'm worried."

"To tell you the truth, Grahm, I'm worried too. Mr. Richmond hasn't mentioned asbestos, but if you're concerned, I'll call him back."

Grahm stood up to leave, "Thanks, Harris. Let me know what he says."

The next day, after noon recess, Room 212's intercom buzzed; it was the school secretary. "Ms. Grahm, are you there?"

"I'm here; we're just back from drinks and the bathroom."

"Good. Mrs. Harris wants to see you in the gym. Mr. Edwards is on his way up to relieve you." A smiling Mr. Edwards strode down the hall toward the room.

*"Why does Harris want to see me in the gym?" she wondered.*

"They're all yours," Grahm turned to Mr. Edwards. "They could use some math 'facts' practice, but do whatever you want. I'll be back as soon as I can." She hurried down the center hall steps to meet the Principal.

Lunch Ladies were cleaning up the lunch clutter; she

could see Mrs. Harris standing at the far side of the gym, near the exit door. She was speaking to someone, obviously NOT a City School employee. While she walked toward them, Grahm scrutinized the 40-something male, wearing a crop of thick — obviously dyed — black hair, slicked back and shiny.

The closer she got, the better she could see his clothing too; black silk stockings, creased, black designer slacks, and Gucci shoes.

"Ms. Grahm, this is Jack De Marco, Chief Electrician on the job. Mr. Richmond sent him over."

"Hello, Mr. De Marco," Grahm responded politely. Up close, she noticed his tanned face and salesman smile. His demeanor reminded her of a mortgage loan officer at a bank.

"Ms. Grahm here is worried about the drilling and the dust…"

*"Harris is putting this ALL this on me. MS. Grahm is worried. Mrs. Harris is NOT?"*

"…especially asbestos fibers."

"You needn't be concerned," he assured them. "Everyone is safe." He patted the first grade teacher on her shoulder.

*"Patronizing too,"* she groaned silently. *"Typical."*

"We have a test for asbestos," he continued. "I just did one for Mrs. Harris here. I'd do another for you, but I don't have any more kits with me. What we are drilling at Robeson is not asbestos. We plan to be finished by Christmas."

"Mr. De Marco and I walked the entire building," interrupted Mrs. Harris. "he says the only asbestos in the building was in the insulation wrapped around the heating pipes, and he has already taken care of that."

While they spoke, the Chief Electrician was steadily inching the three of them toward the outside door.

"I've been in electrical contracting for twenty years; trust me, there is *no* asbestos." He looked directly into their faces and turned on his most reassuring mortgage officer smile.

*"He thinks he's slick. I wonder if Harris believes him?"*

"I'm walking Mr. De Marco to his car," she said. "He's already late for another appointment. I'll meet you in my office."

*"Why is Harris walking him to his car? Shouldn't HE be walking HER to a car?"*

Grahm waited uneasily for Harris' return.

While Harris removed her scarf and leather coat to

hang on a hook behind the door, Grahm noticed her Principal's impassive expression. Her lips were tightly closed. Everything about her reflected 'Downtown Administration'; straightened hair, elaborate jewelry, high heels, and designer clothing. Lately, all her words were noncommittal – politically safe. Grahm remembered when Harris wore jeans and teacher union sweatshirts; she said what she thought and smiled a lot.

*She's changed; she fits in with the rest of the Administration now; wonder why I didn't notice before.*

"Harris, tell me about that *test*."

"Grahm, he crumbled some ceiling tile into a test tube and then he put an eye dropper of some chemical into it and shook it up. It turned red; he said that proved there was no asbestos."

"Did he check anything else?" Grahm asked.

"No, he didn't." "When I asked him to test a floor tile, he got all mad. He said I was insulting his know–how; his experience. That's when I called you, Grahm."

"Are you reassured, Harris?"

"To tell you the truth. NO, I'm not."

*Everyone she ever met, who used the phrase 'to tell you the truth' usually didn't(!) A red flag waved.*

"Harris, I don't trust *any* of them, and I especially

don't trust De Marco or that 'test' today." *And I thought,* *"I'm not sure I can trust you anymore either," which* *made me very sad.*

Harris looked intently at Grahm.

Their eyes met.

*"She REALLY wants me to take care of this, but she* ***dares*** *not say so. She, obviously, feels intimidated by* *Richmond."*

"I'm going to do my best to make it right," Grahm promised her. "I'm not asking your permission; I'm *telling* you what I am going to do. I take total responsibility for this one. YOU are off the hook."

For the second time, Harris' eyes sparkled ever so faintly. She barely nodded in agreement. She said nothing.

Ms. Grahm returned to the second floor. At dismissal, she got her walking students out the front door and the bus riders onto their buses. Upstairs again, she grabbed a ladder from the hall and dragged it inside her room. She cut down a piece of ceiling tile covered with black glue, marked a plastic bag with her room number, and dropped the sample inside. She dragged the ladder back to the hallway, but first scooped up a piece of tile off her classroom floor. That, too, went into a marked plastic bag. She did the same in the hallway. She put a few more baggies into her pocket and headed toward the Preschool room downstairs, where workmen had drilled into floors and ceilings while the teacher, an Aid, and three-year-olds, moved to the other side of the classroom to wait for the dust and drilling, to stop.

The dismayed teacher told Ms. Grahm that workmen returned to drill several more times before they finished, always with her children in the room, watching. Some of her students were only three years old and breathing the dust the drilling raised. She was concerned and pleased that Grahm was willing to try to help them. Grahm also took samples from the kitchen hallway, where dust had been settling on drinking fountains and food for the past week.

Back upstairs in her room, Grahm tucked all the samples inside her briefcase, put a pen in her pocket, made sure she had her checkbook and ID and then drove to a nearby city. She had found a laboratory there, which tested for various contaminants. She had telephoned ahead to make an appointment for this evening.

On the drive to the lab, she had time to think about the enormity of her Cold War. This was a several-million-dollar project she was challenging. Bosses higher than Harris would consider Grahm **THE ENEMY**. For the first time, she was maybe a little scared.

To find the Industrial Parkway address, she drove past many large commercial buildings, across double railroad tracks, and past more buildings to halfway around a *cul de sac* at the far end of the complex. Standing starkly alone, except for a few shrubs on either side of the entrance, was a single-story, yellow brick building; 'Northeast Laboratory', the sign said.

She entered nervously. Briefly, she explained why she was there.

"We don't normally do private testing," the receptionist said.

*Her heart sank.*

*"Keep on talking as if you have done this before,"* she counseled herself. *"Keep your cool."*

"Not to worry," Ms. Grahm continued. "I'll gladly pay upfront; just tell me how much I owe you."

She pulled out her checkbook and the samples from her briefcase. Luckily, she had marked them with numbers, not names. She knew better than to tell this woman they were gathered from public property.

"You have to sign a paper acknowledging you gave

these to us, including today's time and the date. Everyone who handles them does the same. If the results are ever used in a court case, we can prove the chain of custody."

She put Ms. Grahm's sample bags into the lab's sample bags and numbered each one. She typed a description for each sample and had Ms. Grahm sign for each one.

"These should be ready in about three days," she said. "You can pay then."

"I'll expect your call," Grahm smiled. "Thank you very much." On the drive home, Grahm found herself second-guessing;

*"What if there really isn't any asbestos?"*

*"What if you lose your job?"*

*"What if all this effort is for nothing?"*

*"What if there is asbestos and nobody does anything about it?"*

*"Stop it, Grahm!" she ordered.*

A hot shower, clean hair, and a flannel nightgown later, she slept fitfully between short dusty coughs. White ceiling tiles chased her down empty hallways all night.

After dismissal the next day, she toured the building

to take photographs of the places where she had collected samples. When the night cleaning crew pushed their buckets and brooms past her, she pretended to be admiring bulletin boards.

"Good evening, Ms. Grahm. Aren't you here kinda late?"

"I am," she agreed. "We have to get our holiday bulletin boards up; I'm trying to figure out what I want to do."

That *was only half a lie.*

"Good luck, Ms. Grahm; have a good night."

Two days later, there was a message on her answering machine. The lab report was finished. She drove over to pick it up. $120 later, sure enough, there WAS asbestos. Not just in the ceiling tile, but in the 9" X 9" floor tiles in every classroom and in the black mastic which attached the tiles to other surfaces. When conduit had to be installed between floors, the 25% chrysotile asbestos floor tiles were drilled and pried off concrete floors. The 10% asbestos-dried-out mastic became airborne with the tile fragments.

It was time to wage the second step of her COLD WAR; the **LETTER.** During the hour-and-a-half round trip to and from school, it wrote itself.

*Should I send it directly to the District CEO or to my Principal?*

*Let me think. If I send copies RETURN RECEIPT REQUESTED, the original to Harris, my immediate supervisor, then I've given proper notification and followed the proper chain of command. They'll all know at the same time, and each will know that the others know."*

*"Brilliant strategy, Grahm!"* She congratulated herself.

Paul Robeson School
2255 Fifth Avenue
Wednesday, November 29

Dear Mrs. Harris,

Contrary to the Area Superintendent, Mr. Richmond, and the Electric Installers Inc.'s Chief Electrician, there IS asbestos at Robeson School in the 9"X 9" chrysolite asbestos floor tiles and also in the mastic, which adheres them to walls and flooring. Attached is a copy of an independent lab report dated two days ago.

Four days ago, teacher concerns were addressed by an 'expert', who was sent to pacify them by Mr. Richmond. With a test tube, an eye dropper full of an unknown liquid, and a pinch of ceiling tile fragments, this 'expert' shook up the mixture, claiming his test proved there was no asbestos on the Robeson job. From cloudy white, the test tube contents became red in color.

The fox was in the hen house reassuring the chickens! The Company's Chief Electrician (with several million dollars to lose, if the existing asbestos were exposed) was the 'expert'.

However, one hen, unimpressed by foxes, chose to protect her life and lungs (and everyone else's at Robeson) by double-checking several samples of suspicious materials. You now have the results. Construction-related dust, including asbestos fibers, drifts from halls into classrooms and bathrooms and blows into stairwells. Students, staff, and workmen breathe it all day, every day. No safety measures have ever been initiated.

The telephone number for OSHA is 1-800-356-
4674.
I expect that this serious situation will be addressed
immediately.

Sincerely,

L. Grahm, B.A, M.Ed.

cc: Mary Myers Moreno, CEO, AFL/CIO
Teachers' Union, Electric Installers, Inc.

Within hours, exhaust fans, hoses with nozzles to sprinkle down dust, wet mops, and NOA-approved particle masks appeared in every hallway. Drilling was done only at night and on weekends. Construction continued for two more weeks, and the subject of asbestos was never mentioned. On the day Mrs. Harris told Grahm that Myers-Moreno ordered all drilling stopped, conduit was already being installed.

*An 'order' to stop was not needed; the drilling was complete. Did Mr. Richmond hold the Superintendent's order until De Marco told him to release it? Or was the timing of Myers-Moreno's order to coincide with the end of drilling deliberate?*

*Grahm would never know.*

On the night before the final Building Inspection,

ENORMOUS exhaust fans were placed in every hallway on both floors. All windows and doors were opened wide; the fans forced out contaminated air throughout the night. Chrysolite asbestos tiles in every classroom were thoroughly washed, loose ones removed, and the remaining tiles HEAVILY *double* waxed.

Of course, this wiring job by Electrical Installers Inc. passed the Building Inspection with flying colors. Residual dust was removed, insulation was replaced, the air was clean, and the newly installed wiring was up to code. As originally planned, all 400 students could now access their new computers.

*Whatever other side deals were made between the School and the Company could now be completed. Call it paranoia; call it skewed; never again would Grahm trust contractors or administrators. Greed poisoned too many agreements.*

Initially, Grahm was angry - mostly at herself - for not waging a hotter, rowdier war. She had been outwitted. They **were** 'smarter' than her. More experienced, for sure! This wasn't the first time they had dealt with an outraged teacher. Such a one would not be allowed to halt any part of this multi-million dollar deal.

The City Teachers' Union was also noticeably silent about the health concerns **mentioned in her letters**. Apparently, they agreed that asbestos could be dealt with later.

Unfortunately, the children scooted their chairs over the tiles every day, raising asbestos dust as they did so. Grahm could only hope that the double layer of wax held tight. Scooting chairs had been scoring that tile for sixty years. As far as she knew, there had never been a reported case of asbestos poisoning.

What she *didn't know* was that the Company needed only two more weeks to finish the job. The immediate installation of the required fans and sprinklers, and masks bought them said two weeks, while Grahm waited impatiently to hear from Myers-Moreno.

In Grahm's mind, *the CEO* won the Cold War. She was furious at their callous disregard for the students and staff they purported to 'serve'. They deliberately forced children, teenagers, teachers, and other staff, who had to be inside the building to work every day, to breathe asbestos-contaminated air, legally known as 'endangerment'.

The Company's successful Building Inspection of the wiring job brought painfully home to Grahm that 'intelligence' is valuable, but intelligence enhanced by bad experiences is **exponentially MORE** valuable. She was NOT as smart as she thought she was(!) To win a war, one needs to get **inside** the enemy's head. She hadn't learned that when she began her WAR either, but she certainly would never forget it.

Ten years later, with the 20/20 vision of Hindsight, she understood that there was nothing to gain by publicly acknowledging the presence of asbestos at the time of the WAR. Its presence was an overwhelming financial liability that would have destroyed the entire School System. They could not let that happen, and they didn't. Students, along with teachers and other employees would pay the price; they always did.

At least Grahm's COLD WAR had forced conformity to Federal, State, and Industry Health Regulations at the end of the construction. *Some* of the lung damage was averted.

Who knew that double waxed floor tiles could be THE *foundation* of a City Elementary School education!

Like the previous boiler explosion: "WHAT asbestos?"

# 13. JARED

Early one morning in December, Ms. Grahm saw Lorene and her daughter talking seriously in hushed tones outside the kitchen door.

Grahm nodded at them but kept walking. She was making a quick run to her mailbox and needed to return to her room upstairs before the bell rang. She arrived just as Jared and his brother Jarrell were arriving. They often came to school together. Jared hung up his coat, and Jarrell left. Jared seemed tired, and he put his head down on the desk.

"Jared, are you sick?" asked Ms. Grahm.

He didn't answer.

"Does Mrs. Harris know you are here?" (He was on the second day of a three-day suspension. He should have still been at home.)

He looked up at her with wide brown eyes. "My brother got shot."

"Oh, Jared, that's awful. Is he okay?"

"'Yeah. He's alright." He put his head back down on his desk.

"Are you okay?"

"Uh huh."

Jared's foster mother stood at the classroom door. "I've come to get Jared," she said. "His brother was killed, you know. The funeral is tomorrow. He'll be back on Wednesday. His mother will be up to see you."

"Jared, get your things. You're going home."

Ms. Grahm asked, "How are *you* doing through all this?"

"It is very sad," the foster mother answered.

"Bye, Jared," the children chorused.

He gave them a wave of his hand AND disappeared around the corner.

During her free period, while her students were at Library, Grahm sought out Lorene's daughter for some answers. She lived in the Projects, so she would know. Grahm found her outside the Principal's office.

"Excuse me, please." She waited.

"Go ahead," Mrs. Carter answered.

"Jared told me his brother got shot. What happened?"

"Grahm. I wasn't going to talk about it, but you oughta know. Jared is your student." She paused and sighed.

"Remember how warm it was last night? The Project kids was all sitting outside in the courtyard on the playground. When it got dark, a gang from 9<sup>th</sup> Street came in, wearing hoods. Couldn't nobody see who they wuz. Someone opened fire on the kids, and they killed Jared's brother. An then they left."

"Why?" Grahm asked.

"Word in the street says it wuz a turf war goin on."

"Was Jared there?"

"All the kids was there," she said sadly.

"How did that many older kids not get stopped before they got to the Projects?"

"They was really slick. They walked in twos an threes an didn't put their hoods up until they got off the street."

"And you live there, and you have children there; that is scary as hell!"

"You better believe it," she agreed. The parents is gonna do somethin. That jus don make no sense." She shook her head.

"I am so sorry," Grahm said lamely. "Thank you for telling me."

Poor Jared and Jarrell.

On the following Wednesday morning, Jared's biological mother brought him to school. He smiled proudly.

"This is my mom," he announced proudly.

For the next two weeks, Mom took Jared to several appointments.

During those two weeks, Jared was unusually cooperative. The following week, Mom didn't come at all. As a matter of fact, she never came again.

Jared's behavior began to deteriorate. His fellow students were afraid of him, but pretended to like him to avoid his threats and bad temper. Jared was rapidly becoming the class bully. He hit and pushed kids when they didn't do what he wanted, and even called them ugly names.

Finally, one morning he pulled down his sock to show Ms. Grahm a cut on his leg.

"OH, Wow! Jared. How did you get that?" The cut was a clean cut, about two inches long.

"I did it," he said.

"YOU did it? Jared, why?"

"I wanted to be with my brother, but my older brother, he took the knife away."

Ms. Grahm sucked in her breath. Choosing her words carefully, she said, "Jarrell loves you, and I am glad you are still here. Do you need a band-aid?"

"Yeah, I guess."

"I know how it is to be so sad. My daughter was killed."

Jared looked interested.

"Someone killed her in a car wreck on her way home from school."

"I wrote my brother a letter," he said as he pulled a wrinkled paper from his pocket. "Wanna read it?"

"I'd like to read it," answered Ms. Grahm, reaching for the paper.

Other students were quietly gathering close by.

"Der Dan, you wuz nice to me. I wish
I cud be with you.
Luv,
yur bruthr Jared."

"What a heartbreaker!" thought Grahm. "I think your brother is probably looking out for you," she continued. Let's go get your band-aid."

He got the band-aid from the Teacher's Closet and returned to his seat. Grahm walked past the classroom door just in time to see the School Nurse walking toward the office, carrying a huge briefcase stuffed to overflowing. Grahm waved at her to stop.

"Mrs. Johnson, Jared has a cut on his leg which he

says he did to himself. He said he wants to be with his brother."

"Grahm." she said, "We can't let that go."

"I know," said Grahm, "that's why I'm telling you."

"Jared, I need to see you," the Nurse called to him.

Jared walked to her side.

"Let's go talk in my office," she said.

Quietly, Mrs. Johnson said, "I'll call Security. They will send out the Crisis Team. And he will stay with me for now. I'll let you know what happens."

About forty-five minutes later, three men dressed in business suits and carrying briefcases walked past the classroom door. Business suits were not the usual attire for teachers.

On her way out of the building, Mrs. Johnson stopped to update Grahm on Jared. "They determined that the suicide attempt was genuine, but he is not an immediate danger to himself.

"They called in his foster mother and Jarrell too. They worked with the family all day. Jared will need counseling."

"I figured," said Grahm. "I knew you would let me know as soon as you could."

"You know, Grahm, there is so much to do here, and

they schedule me one and a half days a week. Over at the Middle School, I have 1,400 students. I'm there the other two and a half days a week.

"Johnson, you're always smiling. You never act like you are in a hurry. I had no idea you had so many students. Why don't they hire more nurses?"

"I don't think they really care, Grahm. The District is about statistics and dollars, not individual kids' needs. We're tokens to satisfy State Health Departments Regs. The fewer of us they pay, the more money they have to spend elsewhere.

"But they've got football teams and cheerleaders. And buses; those cost money.

"That's good PR, and it brings in more money from the business community."

"Nurses don't, huh?"

She nodded in agreement and changed the subject. "Have a good night!"

"You too."

Jared's behavior became uncontrollable, both at home and at school. His foster mother was afraid of him, and so were the other teachers. All except Grahm. He began to throw things at others and would drop to the floor, rolling around and screaming in frustration when he was corrected or disappointed. He was getting too violent to be safe for himself or others. Juvenile Court finally assigned him to a special residential school for behavior-disordered kids.

# 14. GREAT AMERICAN DREAM

Ms. Grahm was pondering 'success'. There seemed to be so little of it around her. *The more she thought about success, the more she realized she couldn't pin it down; financial success? Academic success? Moral success? Good health? There were too many categories to list.*

Always ready for a good argument, her own intuition finally joined this discussion with herself.

"Great American Dream," it suggested.

"Oh my god! That's IT! THAT'S what I want for my first-graders. *Their* piece of the DREAM, whatever it is. But how do I get them to understand?"

"Talk about the Dream, oh Dense One. Most of them don't know about 'success' except that it is a word they heard once."

*Intuition was not always patient with her. This was a very helpful suggestion; she guessed she'd excuse the insulting language.*

She proceeded, "We're going to talk about a dream," she told her children. "I want you to listen carefully." All seventeen of her first grade students sat taller, watching their teacher with interest.

"Did you ever hear of the American Dream?"

Hands shot up.

"Disney World."

"Yeah, King's Island."

"I'm going to Six Flags this summer."

*Her mind did a 180-degree about-face. The children's Great American Dream was an Amusement Park. Not one child 'dreamed' of anything larger than a good time.*

*Commercial advertising had done its job well. And so had deadly poverty. After all, they **were** only first-graders.*

Mrs. Warren looked up, startled. "I can't believe what I'm hearing, Ms. Grahm." She shook her head. "These kids."

"You're close," their teacher validated. "Going to a theme park *could* be PART of The Dream, but the Great American Dream is about making your WHOLE LIFE what *you want* it to be."

They looked at her quizzically.

"The Great American Dream is, 'If you work very hard, you can be successful'. It doesn't say that you *will* be successful, only that you *can* be successful. The Dream becomes real when *you make* that happen.

"Not everybody *wants* the same kind of life, but everyone wants to FEEL successful. To figure out how they want to be happy and how best to get it. That's the Great American Dream."

*They were attentive. She continued.*

"The more school you finish, the more training you get, and the more likely you are to find a job or open a business that pays the money you want. You may have to work harder to get what you want; you might even have to fight bad people's plans to stop you. But I know how smart you are, and I know for sure that you can figure out how to make The Dream come true for you!

"In first grade, we make our dreams come true by learning to read and write, by learning math and how to solve lots of problems. When we can do that successfully, we can learn how to succeed in all other activities. Success takes practice and sometimes extra help, but we *CAN* do it!"

*Interest was waning; they'd heard all of this before. Well, **most** of it. Grahm was about to lose them; she could see them tuning her out, but she had more to say. She wanted her words to grab their hearts, to imprint their memory, and empower them to build a satisfying future. At the end of this school year, she might never* *see any of these children again. She pressed on.*

"This is why you come to school. This is why I praise you and sometimes even *fuss* at you. What you **do**, *matters* to me. I want you to get your piece of the Great American Dream."

Mrs. Warren, the volunteer, and Senior Citizen Teacher Aid nodded in agreement. "She's right, kids. Listen to her."

*Intuition flashed at her again. These six-year-olds needed motivation, which they could understand and actually MATTERED to THEM.*

"The other side of the 'Dream' is the Great American Nightmare."

*Their interest was pricked. Nightmares and Mary Worth were fascinating and scary topics for all children. Their attention perked up.*

She continued.

"The Nightmare is when someone makes a bad choice and gets sucked into doing drugs or crime or alcohol or worse. It looks like fun at first, but before they know it, they can't hardly make themselves stop doing it. It's a habit almost too hard to break. And it's not *fun* anymore. It's addicting, even dangerous sometimes."

*She HAD 'em! Hands shot up again.*

"My mom smokes reefers wif her frens."

"My gramma puts wine in her coffee cup."

"My mom goes out back with the dog, an she thinks I don't know she smokes Crack back there."

Mrs. Warren's eyebrows rose.

Ms. Grahm searched their faces.

"Do you think that's a Dream or a Nightmare?"

"It's a Nightmare, Ms. Grahm," they answered unanimously.

"So what do you HAVE to do to get *your* piece of the Dream?"

She was prepared for unexpected answers, but instead, she heard her group say in one voice:

"Stay in school!"

"You're RIGHT! Education helps a lot. But what if you don't LIKE school? You don't feel like going anymore?"

She would play the devil's advocate, *knowing full well that someday, that very question would require their serious attention.*

Tashika's hand shot up. "You could make a bad choice and quit," she said.

"I'd stay no matter what," countered Deonte.

"But what if you need money badly?" their teacher prodded.

Everett raised his hand, "You can work and go to school. My mom does." He sat a little taller, proud of his mom.

"My mom don't have hardly no money," said Ronell. "My daddy, he go to the track nearly everday though."

"So what do you want when YOU grow up?" She scanned her students' faces. "The Dream or the Nightmare?"

"I wan the Dream," said Ronell, "an I'm gonna get it, cause I can read," he said proudly.

The children who were now reading and writing agreed, "Yeah, me too!"

*Handsome, clean-cut, quiet King smiled up at his teacher. He had watched this discussion like he had watched every other lesson, unable to follow the conversation. The Dream was premature for him but not necessarily impossible. Ms. Grahm would squeak her wheels long and VERY LOUD for King. The School Psychologist promised to test him next year.*

*Children often made their adults' predictions come true, "You're gonna end up in jail someday." or, "With* those A's, I bet you go to college." She SO wanted them to turn this year's academic success into the driving force behind more achievement, more success.

"You're reading, and you're doing math; you're learning new things. All of you are being successful. You can start *today* to collect some pieces of *your* Great American DREAM. I'm very proud of you!"

William raised his hand.

"Yes, William?"

"Ms. Grahm, can we have Snack now?"

*"Enough, already," intuition counseled. She said no more.*

*She hoped they would remember this day, this talk of Dreams and Nightmares. She hoped each child would stay the path of their own personal success. "**Some** dreams come true," she consoled herself.*

"You bet we'll have Snack, William!"

"Now!"

# 15. SCHOOL YEAR END

On the children's last day of school, Ayesha's mom came to school to pick up Ayesha and her brother. "We have an appointment to see a different apartment at 3:00," she said. "Ayesha, do you have something you want to tell Ms. Grahm?" she asked.

Ayesha looked down at her feet, but she was smiling. "Thank you for being such a nice teacher," she said softly. Her eyes met her teacher's face.

"You're welcome, Ayesha. Did you have a favorite part of first grade?"

Ayesha pondered for a few seconds. "Learning to stick up for myself," she answered. "And reading."

Grahm turned to Ayesha's mother, "Have a great summer," she wished them, "and a great life. I will miss you."

"Thank you, Ms. Grahm; we'll miss you too."

Grahm checked the clock hanging above the door. "The bell will ring in a few minutes, she warned the class. Let's line up."

"Ms. Grahm! Ms. Grahm!" Kara interrupted. She sounded alarmed. "This is the last time we are ever going to line up in first grade!"

"Good grief! I never thought of that. This calls for a group hug, don't you think?" Ms. Grahm opened her arms wide. All her children came running for their hug.

"It's been a great year; I am *really* proud of each of you!" Without arguing or fussing, friends hugged friends. "Remember to read this summer," she reminded them. "Use those library cards."

And the dismissal bell rang so long and loud that her children covered their ears for a few seconds. While they were quiet, she added, "Line up quietly, please." But she figured they probably couldn't; they were too excited.

So she tried again. "If you want to give your old teacher one last present, you could line up quietly."

"Zip it," Pierre warned them. "We're giving her one last present!"

And sure enough, they made that last trip down the stairs as quietly as they could, "YAY," they screamed when they got outside.

This school year was finished. She hadn't realized how heavy the burden of a 'teacher' had become until it was lifted on this last day. Overwhelming relief flooded over her. She waved goodbye until the last yellow bus pulled away. Her children waved back wildly. "See you

155

next year," they shouted.

How many spring times had she said goodbye to children she so carefully tended during the previous school year? For a moment, forgotten faces reappeared. Precious (who wasn't!), Lolita, who threw computers. Tarik, who knelt in penance before his Nigerian mother when she scolded him, Princess Summer and Princess Autumn, who both had Sickle Cell anemia, Willie, who watched drug dealers break into the living room to murder his mother, seven-year-old Tanisha, who had perfect pitch and sang like a professional, James, who knew he was called to be a preacher someday, and Ray Vaugn, who stole everything that wasn't locked away. The list was long, and there would be more every year.

Right now, Ms. Grahm was a Worn Out Warrior. Someday soon, a younger, stronger person would have to take her place in public education. A perpetual summer vacation for the rest of her life sounded glorious and tempting. But she needed to go back upstairs to finish cleaning out her classroom. Tomorrow would be this year's last day of school for teachers.